# DARK PLANET

by

M LeMont

Taylor Green

# Copyright

Copyright ©2022 WH Bone Publishing

ISBN 9798218521240

Cover Design Killercover.com

Table of Content

# Everything is a Revelation

Time binds us all. Everyone's age today is connected to the year 2024. In this moment, the whole world shares the same number.

Your age plus your year of birth equals 2024 for every person. For example, if you're 70 years old and born in 1954, then:

$$70 + 1954 = 2024.$$

This pattern will hold true next year, and the year after that—until we die. In this sense, we are all the same, connected through time.

# WARNING

HILLARY CLINTON ... WARNED
US

"You are the most dangerous person to
ever run

for President in the modern history of
America."

Donald J Trump #45

# Dedication

R.I.P. George Floyd


Justice has been Served


"He did what he did on purpose, and it killed George Floyd," prosecutor said.


We find the defendant guilty your honor on all charges.


Police officer, Derek Chauvin sentenced to 22.5 years in prison.


https://www.youtube.com/watch?v=Q0tEGo7ueNs

# What You Can Expect From This Book

This book is about the prophecy being fulfilled and provides a historical account of how we got here.

The Great American Experiment

The President of the United States

requires no formal education

no experience

bad credit bankruptcy okay

on the job training

4yrs to learn

if you

royally screw up

get impeached twice

incite an insurrection

you get full pay,

pardons, benefits,

bodyguards.

# Blurbs

"A chilling story on DONALD J Trump, told by Satan himself… and a heady mix of history and prophecy." Buzz Pindell


Spellbinding! "Horror is the truth of knowing." TG Berry


A must read. I couldn't stop reading it. "I had to pray afterwards." Connie Roy

# Begin Reading

For God, Yahweh Elohim


I had this dream, a vision of the past,

A paradise where love and beauty last.


The Garden of Eden, where life was
free,

And all of nature danced in harmony.


Stars lit up the sky, and I felt one with
all, a cosmic flow.


No time, no age, no death, just endless
youth, and wealth and status held no
power, no truth.

Everyone was equal, no race, no hate,
And hateful souls had vanished from the
gate.

God spoke to me, "You may eat every
tree,
But not the one of good and evil, see."

The forbidden fruit leads to chaos, pain,
A warning of evil's subtle gain.

But then my soul was lost, my spirit
gone,

As darkness tricked me, sung a siren's
song.

Still, God said, "Rejoice, the day is bright and fair,

Cherish this moment, love, and care."

But the Devil whispers lies in every ear,

And turns our day to rain, doubt, and fear.

Outside, a man stands in front of a church holding the bible for a photo op.

And inside, the preacher is holding a sermon, "the Devil made me do it. The deceiver, the liar, the Prince of Darkness, who twists the truth and leads us to our demise."

The Devil said, "You hear that, that
damn preacher, he's out to get me, and
he'll get you too!"


So much corruption, chaos in the land,
We're lost, like grains of desert sand.


This world is not the heaven that I've
seen,


I've seen in dreams, a thousand times.


I swear to you, I feel it in my soul,
Heaven is where we come from.


But earthly hell is the place where we
live.

I don't know about you, but when I die,
I don't want to see this place again.

# Evil is a Number of a Man

It was all laid out. It happened in 2018 or 2019—I don't remember exactly, but I do recall that #45 was still president. A voice said, "Tell the story." Startled, I replied, "I don't know how." The voice answered, "Don't be dismayed. I will give you the words." And then, I began writing. That's how this book, Dark Planet, came about.

This situation calls for wisdom. It brings to mind a Bible verse that provides valuable insight: Proverbs 4:7 states, "The beginning of wisdom is this: Get wisdom. Though it cost all you have, get understanding."

Isaiah 45:6 — "I am the God of good and evil. I form the light, and create evil.

I alone, and no other, do all these things."


This calls for wisdom. The Bible verse, Isaiah 45:6.


January 6. #45 (6).


Deuteronomy 11:16 — "Take heed to yourselves, that your heart be not deceived, and ye turn aside, and serve other gods, and worship them."


At a Trump rally, a pastor said, "Father, we thank you for our president, Donald J. Trump. Father, we thank you that you used him for your glory…"

Let the one who has insight calculate the number of the beast, for it is the number of a man. That number is 666. ~ Revelation 13:18

The prophecy is being fulfilled. This calls for wisdom.

We're looking at how the number 9 connects to both the number 666 and the 45th President.

First, let's look at 666, the number of the beast from the Bible. If you add the digits together:

$6 + 6 + 6 = 18$, and then break down 18 by adding $1 + 8 = 9$.

Next, for the 45th President, if you add the digits of 45:

$$4 + 5 = 9.$$

Both numbers, 666 and 45, add up to 9.

Interestingly, this also ties back to Isaiah chapter 45 in the Bible. If you add the digits of 45 (the chapter number), you also get:

$$4 + 5 = 9.$$

So, the number 9 appears in 666, the 45th President, and even in Isaiah chapter 45.

There is something about that number 45. Hitler died in 1945. Trump was born in 1946. Evil doesn't die—it reincarnates into another body.

# Prelude

God said, "Suppose ye that I am come to give peace on earth? I tell you, Nay; but rather division: For from henceforth there shall be five in one house divided, three against two, and two against three.

The father shall be divided against the son, and the son against the father; the mother against the daughter, and the daughter against the mother; the mother-in-law against her daughter-in-law, and the daughter-in-law against her mother-in-law."

"Do not think that I came to bring peace on earth. I did not come to bring peace but a sword."

Why are you blinded to these things?


When ye see a cloud rise out of the west,
straightway ye say, "There cometh a
shower," and so it is.


And when ye see the south wind blow,
ye say, "There will be heat," and it
cometh to pass.


"Ye hypocrites, ye can discern the face of
the sky and of the earth, but how is it
that ye do not discern this time? "

# Dark Planet

With the coronavirus killing more than 6 million people worldwide, Sylvia Browne's book End of Days and her predictions are shocking.

She wrote the book in 2008 and said, "In 2020, a severe pneumonia-like illness will spread, killing many people throughout the globe, attacking the lungs and the bronchial tubes…"

She also predicted that, in 2020, a sitting president would die of a heart attack. It made me wonder: what if this is the end of days and she just got the year wrong?

This is 2022, and we're closer now than in 2020. President Joe Biden is 79, Covid mutations like Delta and Omicron are spreading, and the Russia-Ukraine war is ongoing.

The world has become numb, and there is no truth in the land. Everybody is under pressure. Every second that passes feels heavier than we can bear.

The year 2020 was born at midnight on the first day of January.

It began like any other year... 'Wildfires in the Amazon,' 'Kobe Bryant dies in a helicopter crash,' 'Covid-19,' civil unrest, the 'Presidential Election,' and the 'Big Lie.'

Then came 2021: the January 6 attack on the Capitol, the certifying of electoral votes, and Joe Biden becoming president.

I published this book in 2022—it is a work in progress.

The January 6 investigation continues. Russia invades Ukraine, and over 3 million Ukrainian refugees have fled the country. Things are escalating fast.

The world is on the edge of nuclear war.

Vladimir Putin is an evil despot, killing innocent people—women and children.

The world cries out

"My mom called in tears. Her friend, along with the friend's brother and her two children (12 and 2 years old!), were all shot dead by Russian soldiers today while trying to evacuate from Chernihiv.

I don't even know what to say anymore. I'm dying inside."

NATO levies sanctions on Russian banks, oil, and seizes Russian oligarchs' assets.

Zelensky implored NATO to impose a no-fly zone over Ukraine, claiming his country "can beat the aggressor" if Western powers "do their part."

Putin's warning: "Whoever tries to impede us, let alone create threats for

our country and its people, must know
that the Russian response will be
immediate and lead to consequences you
have never seen in history."

That means YOU AND I, AND
EVERYONE ELSE, ARE PROBABLY
GONE. And what if the undead are
awakened and reading this book?

For nearly four years, we drank from the
toxic wellsprings of lies, misinformation,
double-talk, rhetoric, conspiracy theories,
insurrection, and the pandemic—rich
and poor, Black and white, the educated
and uneducated, bureaucrats, scientists,
losers, suckers, and the deranged alike.

Or maybe...

HUMANITY SOMEHOW
SURVIVED.

What follows is a spiritual reckoning.

The war between good and evil.

The story picks up where book one,
Fallen Hero, left off.

Headline: The Supreme Court ruled
Americans no longer have the
constitutional right to an abortion,
erasing a right that's been in place for
almost fifty years.

MY BODY IS NOT MINE IN
AMERICA

Cynthia writes, "Women are being stopped and questioned at state lines! Yet, Kyle Rittenhouse (a minor) carrying an AR-15 across state lines—killing two people—is okay?

Make it make sense!"

What is the abortion ban all about? Greed. Money. Power. Just look at the Census Bureau for answers. The population is declining. Ban abortions, then ban contraceptives. Having more children ensures there are more people enslaved to the system. A new kind of slavery that includes everybody who's not wealthy.

It has nothing to do with God or religion. All under the guise of states' rights and the fervor of Christian Nationalism to control what a woman can do with her body, who you can marry—and it won't stop there. Expect the Voting Rights and Civil Rights Acts to be challenged, and books to be banned from schools to dumb down future generations about the truth and control the narrative.

"The secret of freedom is educating people, whereas the secret of tyranny is in keeping them ignorant." —Maximilien Robespierre

The Confederate States played the long game and waited until they had the right people in place—Supreme Court Justices, state judges, legislators, mayors, and governors. They had planned to take control through politics ever since the Civil War ended in 1865.

Mass Shooting in Texas at Elementary School: 19 students, 2 adults killed.

"The shooter had evil in his heart," Abbott said.

Governor Abbott held a press conference and stated that the police officer who shot the gunman was brave, and the other officers risked their lives.

As the British would say, that's total bull crap.

It took more than an hour before action was taken; 19 officers stood in the hallway outside the classroom because they were scared of being shot.

I am distraught and alarmed over these mass shootings.

I'm sick and tired of it. Three shootings all within 10 days: one in Buffalo, New York, where 10 were killed and 3 injured; a mass shooting in a church in California with 1 dead and 3 injured; and a shooting at a downtown McDonald's in Chicago, where 2 were killed and 3 injured… and now Uvalde, Texas, where 19 children and 2 adults were killed at an elementary school.

A Democratic candidate interrupts the speaker:

"Governor Abbott, I would like to say something… this was totally predictable; we need gun control, and you're doing nothing…"

A staff member yells, "Hey, sit down! Get your ass out of here. This is a press conference."

"Sir, you're out of line."

"Sir, please leave this auditorium!"

A sheriff calls the man, "Sick son of a bitch."

"You are a sick son of a bitch! I can't believe you would come to a deal like this and turn it into a political issue."

America is the Gun Country of the World.

Now we come to a 13-year-old boy named Jack who lives in Virginia. "This is the most astonishing and painfully honest video I've ever seen on buying guns," a viewer says.

MUST SEE: Jack tries to buy beer—rejected. He's a minor. He even tries to buy a lotto ticket—no luck. Then he walks into a gun store and tries to buy an assault rifle… and guess what?

I'll just leave the link here if you can bear to watch it:

https://www.youtube.com/watch?v=fB7MwvqCtlk

Ryan writes, "There is just nothing we can do."

There are two forces at play here— Good & Evil—but one has become more dominant than the other... and the Doomsday Clock remains at 100 seconds to midnight in 2022—the closest ever to apocalypse.

The farthest the clock has been from midnight was 17 minutes. That was in 1991.

Dark Planet, the ragged edge of the universe: COVID-19, corruption, police brutality, racism, protests, mass shootings, and the criminal acts of #45.

# Devil's Message to Man

It's time we had that talk.

You know, the one where you found out
that Santa Claus was your Uncle Billy
and the Tooth Fairy was your momma.

The Devil is in a body and talking
human. The Antichrist is here.

As usual, you don't recognize me. Don't
worry, I'll introduce myself. I will speak
to you as the narrator—in first person,
second person, and sometimes in third
person.

And you will listen.

You watched them all through history: Hitler, Stalin, Putin, Saddam Hussein, Osama Bin Laden, Jim Jones, Charles Manson, Donald Trump, and many more.

Are you confused? Why? It is I, the Devil, who worshipped God for millions of years. I was the greatest of all angels.

I deceived Eve by asking a question and casting doubt: "Did God really say, 'You can't eat from any tree in the garden'?"

I did the same in the 2020 Presidential Election.

I was more crafty, subtle, and shrewd than any beast of the field. I made 25% of the country believe a lie—that the election was stolen and I won by a landslide.

Come with me, and I will show you how I cause corruption in the world and how I manipulate, brainwash, and make people HATE each other, LOSE faith in humanity... and in God.

People want to know what kind of magic I have over the Republican congressmen, my allies, and supporters that made them turn bad. Hell, they were already fucking bad—evil to the core. I just gave them the courage to be themselves.

Let me thank my crew—loyalty means everything.

We almost pulled it off. I want to thank all the coup plotters, crooks, and kooks, lackeys, co-conspirators, and my Republican friends—you are very special: Barr, Meadows, Rudy, Sidney, Bannon, Roger, Kevin, Clark, Marjorie, Gaetz, Nunes, Cruz, Cawthorn, Ginnie, Graham, Brooks, Biggs, Stone, Jordan, Loudermilk, Perry, Alex, Flynn, Eastman, Navarro, Lindell—and Jenna, you tweeted, "The Jan 6 committee is only mad because they can't date me." Yeah, Jenna, fuck that subpoena. Those dumb fuckers. We'll drag that shit out in court.


And Mo Brooks, I loved the line, "We're going to take down names and kick some ass!" That was great, buddy.

Eastman, the Democrats got those emails. You should have burned them. Don't worry—when I get reelected, I'll give you the pardon you wanted. Enjoy your time in prison, John.

Y'all stay strong and don't give in to the radical left Democrats. We won the election by a landslide, and everybody knows it.

# Satan Speaks Out

What kind of magic will you be crafting this full moon evening? A spine of the brave to ravish the world of evil minds, delivering signed copies to every demon in the afterworld and on Earth—a treat of endless torture... Muahahaha! My gift to you.

Listen, come close–I'm singing you a song ♪♫ 'Time is on my side… yes, it is.

You always saying that you want to be free… but in the end, you always come running back to me.'

That's true I do… I always come running back to you. (I come running back to God.)

I want to tell you about my past lives, one in particular.

I'm going to start from the beginning.

You see, old chap, I don't want you to think that I'm making this shit up or lying about anything. Although I do lie…I lie a lot. The media has me lying over 30,000 times in four years.

I'm pretty damn good at lying to people.

I built a fortune on lying. Lying is one of my best virtues, and people love it.  The

National Enquirer published a picture of
an unidentified man having breakfast
with Lee Harvey prior to Oswald
being— you know, shot. Just before
(JFK) was assassinated.

I said it was Meatball Ted Cruz's father. I
mean, the whole thing is ridiculous, I've
never seen Ted's father, but it sure
looked like him.

What was he doing with Lee Harvey
Oswald shortly before the death? Before
the shooting? It's horrible. I had nothing
to do with it. The National Enquirer was
a magazine that, frankly in many
respects, should be very respected. If it
weren't true, they wouldn't have run the
photo. You know what I mean.

My ratings are way up. Have you seen them? Probably not, but that's okay.

You can check them out later. I tell you my life has been bloody hell. I've been here many times before and done a tremendous, amazing job.

I've been a preacher, dictator, king, president, and even a serial killer. When I die, I reincarnate into another body.

Every 5 seconds, a baby's born—plenty of bodies, but I don't have any say to which body I get in.

The Boss takes care of that.

Does that boggle your mind because it does mine?

I can't believe that I'm permitted to talk about this, especially with all the Covid deaths going on.

I'm mainly the cause for neglecting and downplaying the virus, not an entirely easy conclusion to arrive at when I blame everybody else and take no responsibility for anything.

But I guess the end is near, so God's mystery has to be revealed.

Now, let's see, where do I start? I could start at the beginning, but that would take forever. So, let's jump around back and forth in time.

"For in and out, above, about, below,

Tis nothing but a Magic Shadow Show—

Play'd in a Box whose Candle is the Sun,

Round which we Phantom Figures come and go."

There was war in heaven. Michael and his angels fought against the dragon, and the dragon and his angels prevailed not. And the great dragon was cast out of heaven.

That old serpent called the Devil, which deceiveth the whole world was cast out into the earth, and his angels were cast out with him.

That's exactly what happened. Now we're doing the same shit we did in heaven right here on earth-- raising hell.

I got a grand plan, no quick plays. I will ascend above the tops of the clouds; I will be like the Most High.

I will be president one day and rule the world.

I got a brand-new talk, personality, and oratory skills. I will be a great leader.

No need for trick plays, for they will believe whatever I say. I could stand in the middle of Fifth Avenue and shoot somebody and I wouldn't lose any voters… OK? It's like incredible.

I was caught on tape bribing foreign and
US officials NO QUID PRO QUO, I
said.


I did nothing wrong. It's a 'Witch Hunt.'
I even talked about dating women and
some RINO recorded it on video. "I did
try and fuck her. She was married. I
moved on her like a Bitch.


Then all of a sudden, I see her.


You know I'm automatically attracted to
beautiful —just start kissing them. It's
like a magnet. Just kiss. I don't even wait.
Grab 'em by the pussy. They just let me
do it. I can do anything."

That was when I was the Republican candidate running for president. I still won! I have absolute immunity.

I'll give them tokens in exchange for their loyalty and dedication, but it's all for my pleasure. Everyone will be amazed.

Some will call me a powerful man—a great negotiator, and others will call me a stand-in for God.

The people will build great buildings and towers in the sky with my name on them. I'm man's biggest cheerleader.

I nurture his thoughts no matter how perverse they are and give him whatever he wants.

Man thinks he's controlling things, but it's me that's doing it all. It's my own private reality show, and I can't keep from laughing.

I'm streaking toward the finish line, and some will hate me and want to kill me, but that's impossible.

I'm HIDDEN, in bodies until it's time— time to carry out the purpose that I was created for.

I did it in heaven, and I will do it again here on earth.

And the whole time you've seen me walking around as a child, as a man, or woman—dressed in a suit, or wearing a stole around my neck, or maybe as that sweet, caring person you trusted.

And all that time, you didn't know it was me–Satan, the Devil, the Dragon; I go by many names; Lucifer, Beelzebub, Prince of Darkness. Call me whatever you want.

When I bring death and chaos upon the world, you'll hear voices in your head, and just like that, Whoosh! I'll be gone with the SOULS I came for.

This is not a war between Flesh & Blood...

It's a Spiritual War between Good and Evil.

Now I want to tell you about the time I almost died. Many have tried to kill me—gas chamber impossible, electrocution, hanging none of these things phase me, they don't work.

I'm immortal.

They can kill the body, but they can't kill my soul. Only the Boss can do that, and He needs me to carry out His divine purpose. I am Evil Personified --a Worthy Adversary.

Let me begin with a cop that was a pain in my ass…

# Detective Kenneth Fields

"Hi, Mr. Fields…. We're glad to meet you. You know what to do from here."

"Yes, I certainly do."

"You're wired, so we'll be able to hear and record everything."

"I hear the press is coming down pretty hard on the Peoples Temple and I have information that Jim Jones is making plans to flee to Guyana, South America to a compound in the rain forest along with 1,000 of his members.

You know his bodyguards will search me, are you sure we're good?"

"We're good, Mr. Fields. They won't detect a thing."

The story you're about to read is true. The names have been changed to protect the innocent.

This is the city–Los Angeles, California…population 4 million where everything under the sun goes on– evil people and impostors go from bad to worse, deceiving and being deceived.

I work here. I'm a cop, Detective Kenneth Fields, homicide division. I'm also a paranormal investigator.

You may not believe what you're about to hear, at first, I didn't believe it either.

It was April 26, 1976, it was a dull Monday morning that was insipid and lifeless as the weather outside.

I found a business card inside my wife's purse, with a suspicious note scribbled on the back of it. I had my reasons for snooping around.

As a cop with the homicide division, I'm trained to pay attention to everything, to every mundane detail; like how I always look at the license plate when a car passes by or how my mind registers the facial expressions, the dilation of pupils, and overall body language when I'm talking to someone.

Truth is hidden in the things we overlook. A cop knows, a cop sees and thinks over even the most casual things, seemingly oblivious to others.

My wife had been acting rather strange lately; there was a change in her behavior, and she was spending more time at church.

Yes! You heard that right–she was spending a lot of time at church.

Now I don't have anything against religion.

While I consider myself to be a spiritual person, my wife wasn't overly enthusiastic about church or prayer.

It was one of those things that I had to compromise on at the time of our marriage.

But her lack of faith never became a bone of contention in our marriage.

So, it amuses me now, that my formerly less than enthusiastic wife has suddenly become an ardent admirer of a pastor and is always stuck in church! And when she started giving her allegiance to a pastor, whom she fondly called her beloved Father, then something is dreadfully wrong. So I made the call.

"Hello?" he said.

"Can I speak to Randy?"

"Who is this?"

"I'd like to speak to Randy Smith?"

"This is Randy."

"I'm Kenneth Fields–I found a note
with your name on it in my wife's purse.
It said, 'Call me sometimes.' Anyway, my
wife is busy, is there anything I can help
you with?"

"What is your wife's name?"

"Her name is Marsha."

"I don't know any Marsha Fields, so I
guess she never called me," he laughs.

"What is it that you do, Randy Smith?"

"What do you mean? Like what is my occupation?"

"Exactly."

"I'm a minister at the Peoples Temple under our beloved Pastor Jim Jones."

"Is my wife a member of that fake, shenanigan church?"

"Why don't you come see for yourself, Mr. Fields?"

"That's a very tempting offer, I might just do that."

"Okay, then. You got anything else to say?"

"Yea, one other thing. I heard you like cream in your coffee. Is that true?

"Yea, I guess you can say that."

"Well, I like mine black. So, you people better stay the fuck away from my wife, or you'll regret the day you talked to me."

# Strange Things

*"When I say, I am God,*

*then I feel truth well up within my soul."*

The Reverend Jim Jones started the Peoples Temple in Indianapolis in the 1950s.

And in 1965, he relocated to San Francisco, where he became known by his all-day revival meetings.

He bused thousands of people to Los Angeles with promises of faith healings— curing people of cancer, making the blind see and the cripple walk, which later was revealed by insiders as an elaborate hoax to deceive and trick people to join the Temple.

He preached socialism and that everyone could be free and safe from a corrupt capitalistic government that was out to destroy them and that he was building a sanctuary in Guyana, South America.

Once the people became members, they were under his power, and he would have a mental hold over them through mind control, brainwashing, intimidation, and humiliation.

He convinced many followers that he was God reincarnated in a body, and they worshipped and called him Father.

"When I say, I am God,

then I feel truth well up within my soul.

And I see it well up in you,

and I see the sick healed,

and the blind see and the dead raised,"

he shouted in a full-throated roar
in a 1972 sermon.


"You wanna know how I feel? I never
felt so

good when I say I am God." *

Many sold their homes and gave the proceeds to the Temple as gifts, and had their monthly social security checks transferred to the church's foreign bank accounts while they lived in the Temple's facilities.


A member said, "He said he was Gandhi, Buddha, Lenin -- he said he was the coming back of anybody you'd ever want to come back. And we believed him."   *


As New West magazine stated in a publication, titled "Ten Who Quit the Temple Speak Out–"


"It is literally impossible to guess how much money and property people gave Jim Jones in the twelve years since he moved his Peoples Temple to California."

Jim Jones had also become the biggest name in politics; everyone sought his endorsement and his followers' votes.

Some defectors had said that the Peoples Temple was a cult, disguised and operating as a church.

If anyone was found having treasonous thoughts or disobeyed the church's rules, they were punished by being beaten up openly with a wooden paddle, in front of the whole congregation.

It served as a humiliating reminder of the fate of those who sought to betray the church and Jim Jones.

Members who defected were often found dead or missing under mysterious circumstances and apparently with no explanations.

Investigations were secretly underway by the FBI, CIA, and IRS, and local authorities. I often received threatening phone calls and letters to drop the investigation.

The calls would mostly be by men, speaking in baritone voices, and the sentences would almost always begin like this.

"If you value your life or if there's any human being you care about walk away from this case, Mr. Fields."

And I always wanted to say 'I can't do that it's my job and you are hurting innocent people and my wife is one of them.'"

Then there were calls like this one. "Hey, Fields F---- idiot, that's what you are.

You are f---- piece of shit—Trash. Jim Jones was sent here to save the world from people like you.

You dumb motherf----- I'm going to find where you live You---piece of shit ---I can't wait to get my hands on you---"

# Spiritual Reckoning

*God told Satan, "I have raised you up for this very purpose, that I might show my power in you and that my name might be declared in all the earth." Romans 9:17*

My investigation led me to other similar events that occurred in history with similar patterns, though these are off the rational, analytical realm of the real world.

These are deeper spiritual truths mirrored in history, which often repeat themselves after intermittent gaps.

If you look carefully back to the many events that shaped the course of humanity, the evolution of religion & its subsequent influence on society, you'll recognize puzzling patterns.

For every good, there was an equally powerful evil that worked in equal force.

The devil was in the business of holding bodies and minds captive to his vile & foul ideas.

In Cain, the devil sowed the first seeds of evil in the form of immense anger & hatred for his brother Abel; in Pharaoh, he rose as the great dictator who held the Israelites in bondage for 400 years.

A few millennia down the line, he worked himself up as a 20th-century version of Pharaoh, only crueler though short-lived, in the form of Adolf Hitler, who was responsible for the mass genocide of 6 million European Jews between 1933 and 1945.

Hitler once told a journalist in an interview 1922, *"Once I really am in power, my first and foremost task will be the annihilation of the Jews."*

And if you fast forward to 1978, Branch Davidians in Waco, Texas 82 deaths in a Cult Suicide.

The same thing happened in 1997, Heaven's Gate Cult Mass Suicide—39 members committed suicide; their leader Marshall Applewhite preached he was an incarnation of Christ.

But the truth was that he was an incarnation of the Devil himself, HIDDEN in a body.

The members believed all they had to do was shed their earthly body to go to a higher plane of existence.

And let us not forget the crimes committed by Iraq's Saddam Husain in 1999 and Osama Bin Laden and many others.

I know how insane all this might sound, that the Devil can get into a body and grow up as a child and is HIDDEN waiting to wreak havoc on the world.

I wouldn't have believed it myself if I wasn't involved in the investigation of the Peoples Temple case.

Once in power, the evil spirit strikes and commits horrible crimes.

The tragic incidents were not a coincidence.

There was a connection, and the pattern repeated itself at the most convenient time. I had a feeling something terrible was about to happen again.

In 1977 as the authorities were closing in on Jim Jones, he fled the country along with more than 1,000 of his followers to a commune that he called Jonestown.

The Promised Land, as he called it, located in Guyana, South America. It was supposed to be a utopia, a safe haven from the world's bitterness when, in reality, it was nothing more than a concentration camp than anything else.

In November 1978, after complaints from relatives that family members were being held captive, San Francisco Congressman Leo Ryan traveled to Guyana accompanied by reporters and relatives of some Temple members.

The sign read:

*Welcome to the Jonestown Agricultural Project*

When they arrived in the jungle of Guyana and taken to the compound, they met with Jim Jones.

On the surface, everyone seemed to be in paradise, happy and joyous in their new abode.

But the next day, several disgruntled members wanted to return to the US with the Congressman's group.

When everyone boarded the plane and prepared to leave the country, Jonestown's armed guards opened fire and killed the Congressman, three journalists, and one member.

That was the catalyst for Jim Jones to scream over the loudspeakers that the

"White Night" is here and that they were being attacked; it was time for what was his secret weapon—calling for a "revolutionary mass suicide."

They had practiced these sessions many times.

*"White Night! White Night! Get to the pavilion! Run! Your lives are in danger!" Everyone would rush to the pavilion in the middle of the encampment."* *

But this time, it was no dress rehearsal. Jones gathered the group in the center of the compound, and they walked one by one and dipped their cups in a large bin.

That day 909 people died after drinking poisoned Kool-Aid laced with sodium and potassium cyanide. Jim Jones didn't die from the poison—he was found shot in the head.

It was the most harrowing tragedy in American history.

Mass Shootings in America Are Spreading Like a Disease and you think it's just a coincidence?

<u>Twenty-six people shot dead in Sutherland Springs, Texas November 5, 2017</u>

Fifty-nine people shot dead in Las Vegas, Nevada, October 1, 2017.

Forty-nine people shot dead in Orlando, Florida, June 12, 2016.

"Mr. Fields, the FBI, wants to thank you for your undercover work and paranormal investigations. Although the latter is somewhat hard to believe."

"Well, at least, everyone that reads this story will be aware the Devil is HIDDEN in bodies, waiting to strike again, and the only one that can stop him is God.

The things that are happening in the world today is a long spiritual war between GOOD and EVIL, and although we are participants and have to play our roles, the path to salvation depends on the side we find ourselves on."

*We have to ask ourselves, why did 918 people leave this country and go with Jim Jones to Guyana? That's a big question. Why did this group feel they'd rather live in a jungle than in San Francisco, Oakland, Atlanta, wherever they were living? "*"*

There are times that mark your life— when you know things will never be the same.

I was lucky and saved my wife before she got to Jonestown, and I'm sad for those that were not so fortunate.

When you blindly follow a man, that's when destruction begins.

The world filled with deceitful and corrupt people. And for the troubled and the brokenhearted that have something missing in their lives, following a spiritual leader is a one-way ticket to hell, and there's no coming back.

Let us learn from the mistakes of others in search of our happiness and oneness with God.

You might be too young to remember Jonestown or any of the other atrocities that have occurred down through history. But not to be aware is a crime in itself.

Those that cannot remember the past are doomed to repeat it.

Whether you believe what I've uncovered or not, it is irrefutable.

The facts are there for you to delve deeper. Life is a mystery and wrapped up in an enigma impossible to be solved.

There is always something happening, but when it happens, few people see it or understand it or accept it.

You can't see it unless your eyes are open.

It starts with being aware because you're not supposed to know.

It's like the Illuminati, the Mafia, or the Skull and Bones Secret Society they're not supposed to exist, but they do.

Certain phenomena can only be explained if there is a God, and if there are Angels—and they are, they exist. And earth is the battlefield for Good and Evil according to a Divine Purpose, Pattern, and Plan."

"... *the great dragon was cast out of heaven, that old serpent, called the Devil, and Satan, which deceiveth the whole world: he was cast out into the earth, and his angels were cast out with him.*" *

Now that was a fascinating story, and you see why Detective Kenneth Fields was a pain in the ass.

I had to get out of that body as Jim Jones before I was ready. But here's the time that I almost really died.

We have to go back 2,000 years.

Yahshua said, "I saw Lucifer fall from heaven like lightning."

And I heard a loud voice saying in heaven, "Now salvation, strength, and the kingdom of our God, and the power of his Christ have come, for the accuser of our brethren is cast down, which accused them before our God, day and night."

And when Yahshua came to the other side, to the country of the Gadarenes, two demon-possessed men met him, coming out of the tombs, so fierce that no one could pass that way.

And behold, the demons cried out,

"What have you to do with us, O Son of God? Have you come here to torment us before the time?"

Now a herd of many pigs was feeding at some distance from them. And the demons begged him, saying, "If you cast us out, send us away into the herd of pigs."

And Yahshua said to them, "Go." So they came out and went into the pigs, and behold. The whole herd rushed down the steep bank into the sea and drowned in the waters.

That was the time I almost died.

God could have sent me straight to hell, but instead, he sent me into the bodies of a herd of swine so I could reincarnate.

I'm to rule the earth for 4,000 years—and the day of reckoning is fast approaching.

The war between GOOD and EVIL is a fixed fight—it's not meant for me to win.

I'll have to pay for all the destruction that I've brought upon humanity.

Right now, I'm bidding my time, and I will strike soon rather soon, I believe, as another great leader. And remember when a mother gives birth, and the doctor spanks the newborn, you'll hear the baby cry--that will be me.

Until then, peace be with you, and look out-- I will be great again.

Donald John Trump appeared in a human body on June 14, 1946, in Queens, New York, to the parents of Fred, a real estate developer, and his wife, Mary.

Trump attended private school in Queens and later enrolled in the New York Military Academy. After college, he joined his father's company and developed apartments in New York City.

He became president of the firm in 1974. Later he went on to build a real estate empire in Manhattan-- The Grand Hyatt hotel in New York and Trump Tower and starred in the TV reality show The Apprentice for 14 seasons. The rest is history.

# Pure Evil

George Washington predicted,

that cunning, ambitious, and
unprincipled

men will be enabled

to subvert the power of the people and

to usurp for themselves the reins of
government.

What happened in 2016?

How did Donald Trump get elected president?

How could America let an insurrection happen and never hold him and his coconspirators accountable?

The story continues. Let us trace Satan to Hitler in the Nuremberg trials in Germany, 1945.

# November 21, 1945

The parallelism between Adolf Hitler and Donald Trump is frightening. In 1923, Adolf Hitler led a failed coup. He was treated leniently. Germany moved on. A decade later, he was elected, and the atrocities of the world ensued. We must not move on. We must not forget, or history will repeat itself. — A Microcosm.

On January 6, 2021, Donald Trump led a failed coup. The Republican party called it 'Legitimate Political Discourse.' A tourist attraction.

President Joe Biden addressed the nation on September 1, 2022: "Donald Trump and the MAGA Republicans represent extremism that threatens the very foundations of our republic. MAGA Republicans have made their choice. They embrace anger. They thrive on chaos. They live not in the light of truth but in the shadow of lies."

Not every Republican embraces their extreme ideology. I know because I've been able to work with these mainstream Republicans," Biden said. "But there's no question that the Republican Party today is dominated, driven and intimidated by Donald Trump and the MAGA Republicans, and that is a threat to this country."

**The International Military Tribunal, November 21, 1945.**


Justice Robert H Jackson, Chief Counsel for the United States of America, opening statement.


May it please, Your Honors:

The privilege of opening the first trial in history for crimes against the peace of the world imposes a grave responsibility.

The wrongs which we seek to condemn and punish have been so calculated, so malignant, and so devastating, that civilization cannot tolerate their being ignored, because it cannot survive their being repeated.

That four great nations, flushed with victory and stung with injury stay the hand of vengeance and voluntarily submit their captive enemies to the judgment of the law is one of the most significant tributes that Power has ever paid to Reason.

Less than 8 months ago today the courtroom in which you sit was an enemy fortress in the hands of German SS troops.

 Less than 8 months ago nearly all our witnesses and documents were in enemy hands.

The law had not been codified, no procedures had been established, no tribunal was in existence, no usable courthouse stood here, none of the hundreds of tons of official German documents had been examined, no prosecuting staff had been assembled, nearly all of the present defendants were at large, and the four prosecuting powers had not yet joined in common cause to try them.

"The common sense of mankind demands that law shall not stop with punishment of petty crimes by little people. It must also reach men who possess great power make deliberate use to set in motion evils which, leave no home in the world untouched."  (Nov 21, 1945)


"In the prisoners' dock sit twenty-odd broken men. Reproached by the humiliation of those they have led almost as bitterly as, by the desolation of those they have attacked, their personal capacity for evil is forever past."


"It is hard now to perceive in these men as captives the power by which as Nazi leaders they once dominated much of the world and terrified most of it. Merely

as individuals, their fate is of little
consequence to the world."

"What makes this inquest significant is
that these prisoners represent sinister
influences that will lurk in the world long
after their bodies have returned to dust."

"We will show them to be living symbols
of racial hatreds, of terrorism and
violence, and of the arrogance and
cruelty of power. They are symbols of
fierce nationalisms, militarism, intrigue &
war-making which have embroiled
Europe generation after generation."

"They have identified themselves with
the philosophies they conceived and with
the forces they directed that any
tenderness to them is a victory and an

encouragement to all the evils attached
to their names."


"Civilization can afford no compromise
with the social forces which would gain
renewed strength if we deal ambiguously
or indecisively with the men in whom
those forces now precariously survive."
(Nov 21, 1945)


"What these men stand for we will
patiently and temperately disclose. We
will give you undeniable proof of
incredible events. The catalog of crimes
will omit nothing that could be
conceived by a pathological pride,
cruelty, and lust for power."

No greater mistake could be made than to think of the Nazi Party in terms of the loose organizations which we of the western world call "political parties".

In discipline, structure, and method the Nazi Party was not adapted to the democratic process of persuasion. It was an instrument of conspiracy and of coercion.

The Party was not organized to take over power in the German State by winning support of a majority of the German people; it was organized to seize power in defiance of the will of the people.

The Nazi Party, under the "Führerprinzip," was bound by an iron discipline into a pyramid, with the

Führer, Adolf Hitler, at the top and broadening into a numerous Leadership Corps, composed of overlords of a very extensive Party membership at the base.

By no means all of those who may have supported the movement in one way or another were actual Party members.

The membership took the Party oath which in effect amounted to an abdication of personal intelligence and moral responsibility.

This was the oath: "I vow inviolable fidelity to Adolf Hitler; I vow absolute obedience to him and to the leaders he designates for me."

The membership in daily practice followed its leaders with an idolatry and self-surrender more Oriental than Western.

That four great nations, flushed with victory and stung with injury stay the hand of vengeance and voluntarily submit their captive enemies to the judgment of the law is one of the most significant tributes that Power has ever paid to Reason.

This Tribunal, while it is novel and experimental, is not the product of abstract speculations nor is it created to vindicate legalistic theories.

This inquest represents the practical effort of four of the most mighty of nations, with the support of 17 more, to utilize international law to meet the greatest menace of our times-aggressive war.

It is a cause of that magnitude that the United Nations will lay before Your Honors.

They took from the German people all those dignities and freedoms that we hold natural and inalienable rights in every human being.

The people were compensated by inflaming and gratifying hatreds towards those who were marked as "scapegoats".

Against their opponents, including Jews, Catholics, and free labor, the Nazis directed such a campaign of arrogance, brutality, and annihilation as the world has not witnessed since the pre-Christian ages.

They excited the German ambition to be a "master race", which of course implies serfdom for others. They led their people on a mad gamble for domination.

They diverted social energies and resources to the creation of what they thought to be an invincible war machine.

They overran their neighbors.

To sustain the "master race" in its war-making, they enslaved millions of human beings and brought them into Germany, where these hapless creatures now wander as "displaced persons".

At length bestiality and bad faith reached such excess that they aroused the sleeping strength of imperiled Civilization.

Its united efforts have ground the German war machine to fragments. But the struggle has left Europe a liberated yet prostrate land where a demoralized society struggles to survive.

These are the fruits of the sinister forces that sit with these defendants in the prisoners' dock

.

At the very outset, let us dispose of the contention that to put these men to trial is to do them an injustice entitling them to some special consideration. These defendants may be hard pressed but they are not ill used. Let us see what alternative they would have to being tried.

More than a majority of these prisoners surrendered to or were tracked down by the forces of the United States. Could they expect us to make American custody a shelter for our enemies against the just wrath of our Allies?

Did we spend American lives to capture them only to save them from punishment?

If these defendants should succeed, for any reason, in escaping the condemnation of this Tribunal, or if they obstruct or abort this trial, those who are American-held prisoners will be delivered up to our continental Allies.

For these defendants, however, we have set up an International Tribunal and have undertaken the burden of participating in a complicated effort to give them fair and dispassionate hearings. That is the best-known protection to any man with a defense worthy of being heard.

If these men are the first war leaders of a defeated nation to be prosecuted in the name of the law, they are also the first to be given a chance to plead for their lives in the name of the law.

Realistically, the Charter of this Tribunal, which gives them a hearing, is also the source of their only hope.

It may be that these men of troubled conscience, whose only wish is that the world forget them, do not regard a trial as a favor.

But they do have a fair opportunity to defend themselves-a favor which these men, when in power, rarely extended to their fellow countrymen.

Despite the fact that public opinion already condemns their acts, we agree that here they must be given a presumption of innocence, and we accept the burden of proving criminal acts and the responsibility of these defendants for their commission.

When I say that we do not ask for convictions unless we prove crime, I do not mean mere technical or incidental transgression of international conventions.

We charge guilt on planned and intended conduct that involves moral as well as legal wrong. And we do not mean conduct that is a natural and human, even if illegal, cutting of corners, such as many of us might well have committed had we been in the defendants' positions.

It is not because they yielded to the normal frailties of human beings that we accuse them. It is their abnormal and inhuman conduct which brings them to this bar.

We will not ask you to convict these men on the testimony of their foes. There is no count in the Indictment that cannot be proved by books and records.

The Germans were always meticulous record keepers, and these defendants had their share of the Teutonic passion for thoroughness in putting things on paper.

Nor were they without vanity. They arranged frequently to be photographed in action. We will show you their own films.

You will see their own conduct and hear their own voices as these defendants re-enact for you, from the screen, some of the events in the course of the conspiracy.

We would also make clear that we have no purpose to incriminate the whole German people.

We know that the Nazi Party was not put in power by a majority of the German vote.

We know it came to power by an evil alliance between the most extreme of the Nazi revolutionists, the most unrestrained of the German reactionaries, and the most aggressive of the German militarists.

If the German populace had willingly accepted the Nazi program, no Storm-troopers would have been needed in the early days of the Party and there would have been no need for concentration camps or the Gestapo, both of which institutions were inaugurated as soon as the Nazis gained control of the German State.

Only after these lawless innovations proved successful at home were they taken abroad.

The German people should know by now that the people of the United States hold them in no fear, and in no hate.

It is true that the Germans have taught us the horrors of modern warfare, but the ruin that lies from the Rhine to the Danube shows that we, like our Allies, have not been dull pupils.

If we are not awed by German fortitude and proficiency in war, and if we are not persuaded of their political maturity, we do respect their skill in the arts of peace, their technical competence, and the sober, industrious, and self-disciplined character of the masses of the German people.

In 1933 we saw the German people recovering prestige in the commercial, industrial, and artistic world after the set-back of the last war.

We beheld their progress neither with envy nor malice. The Nazi regime interrupted this advance.

The recoil of the Nazi aggression has left Germany in ruins.

The Nazi readiness to pledge the German word without hesitation and to break it without shame has fastened upon German diplomacy a reputation for duplicity that will handicap it for years.

Nazi arrogance has made the boast of the "master race" a taunt that will be thrown at Germans the world over for generations.

The Nazi nightmare has given the German name a new and sinister significance throughout the world which will retard Germany a century.

The German, no less than the non-German world, has accounts to settle with these defendants.

The fact of the war and the course of the war, which is the central theme of our case, is history.

I now come to "Crimes against the Jews."

TO PRESIDENT: We shall now take our noon recess.

[A recess was taken until 1400 hours.]

THE PRESIDENT: The Tribunal will adjourn for 15 minutes at half past 3 and will then continue until half past 4.

MR. JUSTICE JACKSON: I was about to take up the "Crimes Committed against the Jews."

The most savage and numerous crimes planned and committed by the Nazis were those against the Jews.

Those in Germany in 1933 numbered about 500,000. In the aggregate, they had made for themselves positions which excited envy, and had accumulated properties which excited the avarice of the Nazis.

They were few enough to be helpless
and numerous enough to be held up as a
menace.

Let there be no misunderstanding about
the charge of persecuting Jews.

What we charge against these defendants
is not those arrogances and pretensions
which frequently accompany the
intermingling of different peoples and
which are likely, despite the honest
efforts of government, to produce
regrettable crimes and convulsions.

It is my purpose to show a plan and
design, to which all Nazis were
fanatically committed, to annihilate all
Jewish people.

These crimes were organized and promoted by the Party leadership, executed and protected by the Nazi officials, as we shall convince you by written orders of the Secret State Police itself.

The persecution of the Jews was a continuous and deliberate policy.

It was a policy directed against other nations as well as against the Jews themselves.

Anti-Semitism was promoted to divide and embitter the democratic peoples and to soften their resistance to the Nazi aggression. As Robert Ley declared in Der Angriff on 14 May 1944:

"The second German secret weapon is Anti-Semitism because if it is constantly pursued by Germany, it will become a universal problem which all nations will be forced to consider."

Anti-Semitism also has been aptly credited with being a "spearhead of terror."

The ghetto was the laboratory for testing repressive measures. Jewish property was the first to be expropriated, but the custom grew and included similar measures against anti-Nazi Germans, Poles, Czechs, Frenchmen, and Belgians.

Extermination of the Jews enabled the Nazis to bring a practiced hand to similar measures against Poles, Serbs, and Greeks.

The plight of the Jew was a constant threat to opposition, or discontent among other elements of Europe's population-pacifists, conservatives, Communists, Catholics, Protestants, Socialists.

It was in fact, a threat to every dissenting opinion and to every non-Nazi's life.

The persecution policy against the Jews commenced with nonviolent measures, such as disfranchisement and discriminations against their religion, and the placing of impediments in the way of success in economic life.

It moved rapidly to organized mass violence against them, physical isolation in ghettos, deportation, forced labor, mass starvation, and extermination.

The Government, the Party formations indicted before you as criminal organizations, the Secret State Police, the Army, private and semi-public associations, and "spontaneous" mobs that were carefully inspired from official sources, were all agencies that were concerned in this persecution.

Nor was it directed against individual Jews for personal bad citizenship or unpopularity.

The avowed purpose was the destruction of the Jewish people as a whole, as an end in itself, as a measure of preparation for war, and as a discipline of conquered peoples.

The conspiracy or common plan to exterminate the Jew was so methodically and thoroughly pursued, that despite the German defeat and Nazi prostration this Nazi aim largely has succeeded.

Only remnants of the European Jewish population remain in Germany, in the countries which Germany occupied, and in those which were her satellites or collaborators.

Of the 9,600,000 Jews who lived in Nazi-dominated Europe, 60 percent are

authoritatively estimated to have
perished."

"Five million seven hundred thousand
Jews are missing from the countries in
which they formerly lived, and over
4,500,000 cannot be accounted for by
the normal death rate nor by
immigration; nor are they included
among displaced persons."

History does not record a crime ever
perpetrated against so many victims or
one ever carried out with such calculated
cruelty."

"You will have difficulty, as I have, to
look into the faces of these defendants
and believe that in

this twentieth century human beings could indict such sufferings as will be proved here on their own countrymen as well as upon their so-called "inferior" enemies.

Particular crimes, and the responsibility of defendants for them, are to be dealt with by the Soviet Government's counsel, when committed in

the East, and by counsel for the Republic of France when committed in the West.

I advert to them only to show their magnitude as evidence of a purpose and a knowledge common to an defendants, of an official plan rather than of a capricious policy of some individual commander, and to show such a continuity of Jewish persecution from the rise of the Nazi conspiracy to its collapse as forbids us to believe that any person could be identified with any part of Nazi action without approving this most conspicuous item in their program."


"It is also not only a European problem!


The Jewish question is a world question!


Not only is Germany not safe in the face of the Jews as long as one Jew lives in Europe,


but a so the Jewish question is hardly solved in Europe so long as Jews live in the rest of the world."

[The Tribunal adjourned until 22
November 1945 at 1000 hours.]


https://www.roberthjackson.org/speech
-and-writing/opening-statement-before-
the-international-military-tribunal/

# Fast Forward to 2021

Donald J Trump

When you trust one man above all else, science, medical experts, news networks, and federal agencies defy your own common sense and well-being. When you believe that one man, whatever he says—you are fully indoctrinated into a cult.

"I did what my President told me to do.

 I'm sad. I thought he would give us a pardon."

What do you have to say Mr. President? "I have nothing to hide," Trump said. "I wasn't involved in that and if you look at my words and what I said in the speech, they were extremely calming, actually."

Trump, "We won with the Evangelicals we won with young we won with old we won with highly educated we won with poorly educated 'I love the poorly uneducated' most loyal people..."

Stupidity is my opportunity.

Adam Schiff Closing Speech Impeachment Trial: 'Is there one among you who will say, Enough!'?

"We must say enough — enough!

He has betrayed our national security; he will do so again.

He has compromised our elections. You will not change him.

You cannot constrain him. He is who he is. Truth matters little to him. What's right matters even less, and decency matters not at all."

"You are decent," he added. "He is not who you are."

And then on Jan 30, 2022 ... "If I run and I win, we will treat those people from Jan. 6 fairly," Trump said, at a rally in Conroe, Texas outside Houston, that appeared to number in the tens of thousands.

"We will treat them fairly," he repeated.

"And if it requires pardons, we will give them pardons, because they are being treated so unfairly."

At least 700 people were arrested in connection with the Jan. 6 insurrection, including 11 who have been charged with seditious conspiracy.

Some have said they believed Trump was their Savior and would do anything for him.

Guy Reffitt, a 49-year-old was sentenced to 7 ¼ years for his part in the Jan. 6 insurrection. He was a recruiter for the militant group the Three-Percenters. A jury found him guilty on five counts: two counts of civil disorder and one count each of obstruction of an official proceeding, entering and remaining on restricted grounds with a firearm and obstruction of justice.

After the trial his daughters spoke out. "To mark my dad as this horrible person, and then having him prosecuted like this, when somebody is maybe even able to get elected again? Doesn't seem right to me," Sarah Reffitt said.

"Trump deserves life in prison if my father is in prison for this long," Peyton Reffitt said. "President Trump deceived my father and many other normal citizens with families to believe that this past election was fraudulent," the 18-year-old wrote, via CNBC.

Speaking in court during the trial, Peyton Reffitt denied that her father was leading the riot on January 6. "My father's name wasn't on all the flags that were there that day, that everyone was carrying," she said. "It was another man's name."
Trump!

# Mocking God

Trump deployed police & national
guards on peaceful protestors to pave
the way for his photo opt in front of St.
John's Episcopal Church holding the
Bible upside down


"I am your president of Law and Order
and ally of all peaceful protestors."


https://www.youtube.com/watch?v=Jx
YmILDya0A


  An interviewer tried asking Trump what
his favorite bible scripture was, but he
didn't want to discuss it.

Trump said he wouldn't want to get into it because it's very personal and the bible means a lot to him.

https://www.youtube.com/watch?v=ERUngQUCsyE

https://twitter.com/MisterSalesman/status/1536028347213524992

Mayor Bowser, Mayor of Washington DC to paint BLACK LIVES MATTER MURAL ON STREETS LEADING TO WHITE HOUSE in response to photo opt by Donald Trump in front of church…

https://twitter.com/MisterSalesman/status/1353590577208717312

# The Nixon-Trump Connection

Have you no sense of decency sir …

at long last have you left no

sense of decency. Joseph Welch, Chief
Counsel US Army 1954

Donald Trump and Richard Nixon
wrote letters to each other in the 1980s.
The letters are kept in the Richard Nixon
Presidential Library & Museum.

https://www.politico.com/news/2020/
09/23/donald-trump-richard-nixon-pen-
pals-420567

Pen pals?  Well, I have another angle for
the story.  The same spirit in Nixon was

in Trump, and Trump studied and admired Nixon while in office.  See the WORDS, the PATTERNS, and the SIMILARITIES.

Here's a side-by-side analysis. *Richard Nixon quotes via Daniel Kurtzman at liveabout

If Twitter were around in his day, Nixon would have used it just as much as Donald Trump.

"Voters quickly forget what a man says."
—President Richard Nixon

"So you have evidence of 400K illegal immigrants and dead people voting? Will you give it to me?"  Trump says, 'Give the man what he needs Rudy.'  Bowers,

"I never got it."—Rusty Bowers AZ testimony about Rudy Giuliani's call to overturn election


"When the President does it, that means it's not illegal." —President Richard Nixon, in a 1977 interview with David Frost


"You don't know how to lie. If you can't lie, you'll never go anywhere." —President Richard Nixon, giving advice to a political associate


Donald Trump: "We won the election This is a fraud on the American public This is an embarrassment to our country."

"I was not lying. I said things that later on seemed to be untrue." —President Richard Nixon, reflecting on the Watergate scandal in 1978

Donald Trump: "We won states and all of a sudden, what happened to the election? It's off … All of a sudden everything just stopped."

"I can say categorically that his investigation indicates that no one on the White House staff, no one in this administration, presently employed, was involved in this very bizarre incident [the Watergate burglary].

What really hurts in matters of this sort is not the fact that they occur, because overzealous people in campaigns do things that are wrong. What really hurts is if you try to cover it up." —President Richard Nixon at the beginning of the Watergate scandal

Trump: I would like you to do us a favor I would like you to find out what happened whole situation with Ukraine they say Crowdstrike the server They say Ukraine has it That whole nonsense ended very poor performance by man named Robert Mueller an incompetent" —Trump bribing Ukraine President

"I was under medication when I made the decision to burn the tapes." — President Richard Nixon

"I don't F'cking care that they have weapons. They're not here to hurt me. Take the mags away. Let my people in." — Trump told staffers about crowd on Jan 6

"People have got to know whether or not their President is a crook. Well, I'm not a crook. I've earned everything I've got."—President Richard Nixon at a November 17, 1973 news conference

Judicial Oversight Committee: "To your knowledge, did the president or his company ever inflate assets or revenues?" Michael Cohen: Yes. "Was that done at the president's knowledge and direction?" Yes, everything was done with the knowledge & direction of Mr. Trump. —Michael Cohen, Trump's lawyer and fixer testifies against Donald Trump.


"I urge the Congress to join me in mounting a major new effort to replace the discredited president." —President Richard Nixon, in his 1974 State of the Union address at the height of the Watergate scandal, fumbling a line in which he meant to say "replace the discredited present system"


Trump: "If Biden somehow manages to win this election, you won't see me again, I'll leave the country!"


"I want to make sure he is a ruthless son of a bitch, do what he's told, that every income tax I want to see I see, that he will go after our enemies and not our friends. Now it's as simple as that. If he doesn't he doesn't get the job." — President Richard Nixon, on appointing an IRS commissioner


Trump: "If you see somebody getting ready to throw a tomato, knock the crap out of them, would u? Seriously OK? Just knock the hell I promise I'll pay legal fees Look he's walking out smiling I'd like to punch him in the face." —Trump at rally telling the crowd if they see any hecklers, to knock the shit out of them.


"I don't give a s**t what happens. I want you all to stonewall—plead the Fifth Amendment, cover-up, or anything else. If that will save it, save the plan." —— President Richard Nixon to his subordinates in the White House during Watergate

Trump: "I had an election Rigged and Stolen from me, and our Country. The USA is going to Hell," —Trump wrote after the FBI search his home after midnight. "Am I supposed to be happy?"

"Goddamn it, get in and get those files. Blow the safe and get them. The way I want that handled is…just to break in. Break in and take it out! You understand? … You are to break into the place, rifle the files, and bring them out…Just go in and take it! Go in around eight or nine o'clock. And clean it up." —President Richard Nixon in 1971, ordering his chief of staff, H.R. Haldemann

Trump: "I only need 11,000 votes - fellas, I need 11,000 votes," Trump said on the Georgia call. "Give me a break.

You know we have that in spades already." —Trump phone call to GA Secretary of GA to throw away votes.

"I'm not for women in any job. I don't want any of them around. Thank God we don't have any in the cabinet." —President Richard Nixon in a taped 1971 conversation with his chief of staff

Trump: "She's bad news. This was not an angel, this woman, okay? And there were a lot of things that she did that I didn't like, she's a woman - we have to be nice." —Trump talking about Marie Yovanovitch, former ambassador to Ukraine.

"Sure, there are dishonest men in local government. But there are dishonest

men in national government too." —
President Richard Nixon


Trump: "Can't you just shoot them? Just
shoot them in the legs or something?"
—Trump said about George Floyd's
Protestors to Secretary of Defense, Mark
Esper.


"It is the responsibility of the media to
look at the President with a microscope,
but they go too far when they use a
proctoscope." —President Richard
Nixon


Trump: "They can make anything bad,
because they are the fake, fake,
disgusting news." —

Trump: "We were way up in Pennsylvania, and it was only 2% of the vote left and if we lost every vote, we were way up if I lost every vote, we would have won the state of Pennsylvania and the "Fake News" refused to call it…. right" —Trump at a rally pushing the Big Lie


"When I grow up, I want to be an honest lawyer so things like that (the Teapot Dome scandal) can't happen." —President Richard Nixon


"Do you know what happened to the Romans? The last six Roman emperors were fags....You know what happened to the Popes? It's all right that Popes were laying the nuns, that's been going on for years, centuries, but, when the popes, when the Catholic Church went to hell, in, I don't know, three or four centuries ago, it was homosexual." —President Richard Nixon

In a tape-recorded 1972 Oval Office conversation between President Richard

Nixon and Rev. Billy Graham, the nation's best-known preacher agreed with a stream of bigoted comments Nixon made about Jews and their perceived influence in American life.

Graham: "This stranglehold (of Jews in the media) has got to be broken or the country's going down the drain."

Nixon: "You believe that?"

Graham: "Yes, sir."

Nixon: "Oh, boy. So do I. I can't ever say that but I believe it." Graham: "No, but if you get elected a second time, then we might be able to do something."

Trump: "I don't know Putin I have no deals in Russia, and the haters are going crazy—yet Obama can make a deal with Iran #1 in terror no problem!"—Donald Trump 2/7/2017

"You know, it's a funny thing. Every one of the bastards that are out for legalizing marijuana is Jewish. What the Christ is the matter with the Jews, Bob? What is the matter with them? I suppose it is because most of them are psychiatrists."

—President Richard Nixon to White House Chief of Staff Bob Haldeman

"The real scandal here is that classified information is illegally given out by "intelligence" like candy. Very un-American!" —Trump tweeted on Feb. 15, 2017

"I think we ought to move tanks, the whole goddamned thing. Put a division in there, if necessary, It's time for action on it. If some Indians get shot, that's too goddamned bad. If some Americans get shot, that's too bad, too." —President Richard Nixon on the standoff at Wounded Knee with Native American militants

Trump: "Look, I don't want any wounded guys in the parade. This doesn't look good for me." Kelly: "Those are the heroes. Trump: "I don't want them."


"As I leave you, I want you to know—just think how much you're going to be losing--you won't have Nixon to kick around anymore, because, gentlemen, this is my last press conference." — Richard Nixon to the press in 1962 after losing the California election for governor


Trump: "The movement we started is only just beginning. There has never been anything like it… I came to Washington as the only true outsider to ever win the presidency." —Trump's Farewell Address to the Nation.

"Reagan is not one that wears well. On a personal basis, Rockefeller is a pretty nice guy, Reagan on a personal basis, is terrible. He just isn't pleasant to be around. He's just an uncomfortable man to be around...strange." —President Richard Nixon in 1972

Trump: "An 'extremely credible source' has called my office and told me that Barack Obama's birth certificate is a fraud," — Another bald-faced lie Trump tweeted in August 2012.

"I'm not going to be the first American president to lose a war." —President Richard Nixon in October 1969, six years before the Vietnam War finally ended.

Trump:  I am really happy with the job we're doing and I'm glad this team and me are here for this horrible thing… I mean a number of people have said it and I feel it actually… I'm a "Wartime President."


"It is necessary for me to establish a winner image. Therefore, I have to beat somebody." —President Richard Nixon


Trump:  "My two greatest assets have been mental stability and being, like, really smart," a 'Very Stable Genius' — Trump tweeted in 2018


"Solutions are not the answer." — President Richard Nixon

Trump: "I went from VERY successful businessman, to top T.V. Star....." — Trump tweeted in 2018.

"Politics would be a helluva good business if it weren't for the goddamned people." —President Richard Nixon

"You know, I always wondered about that taping equipment but I'm damn glad we have it, aren't you?"—President Richard Nixon to Watergate co-conspirator H.R. Haldeman in April 1973, weeks before the Senate began its hearings

Reporter: "Let me ask you, Mr. President, why did you wait so long to blast neo-Nazis?"

Trump: "I didn't wait long. I didn't wait long."

Reporter: "Forty-eight hours.

"Trump:  "You look at what I said, you will see that that question was answered perfectly. And I was talking about people that went because they felt very strongly. —Trump's refusal to denounce White Supremacist groups in Charlottesville rally in 2019

During the Presidential debate in 2020 Trump talks in code to the White Supremacists group the Proud Boys and tells them to wait for further instructions.


Chris Wallace: Are you willing tonight to condemn White Supremacists and militia groups?


Trump: "Sure I'm willing to do that."
Biden: Then do it, say it, say it ... "Uh what do you want to call them?" You know.  "Proud Boys.  Stand Back and Stand By."


https://www.youtube.com/watch?v=JZk6VzSLe4Y

# The Big Lie was Born

We must keep "evil" out of our country!
— Donald Trump, Feb 3, 2017

According to a Post report, Donald Trump told 30,000 lies in four years. That's about 21 lies per day. For if a lie is believed for only an hour, it has done its work, and if it's repeated constantly, more people will believe it.

Trump: "So, supposing we hit the body with ultraviolet or just very powerful light & then I see the disinfectant where it knocks it out in a minute, I think you said you're going to test it." —Trump asked Dr. Birx about injecting disinfection to cure Covid.

Then there was the time when Trump declared himself to be a wartime President: to fight off the invisible enemy. (Covid) "I mean a number of people have said it and I feel it actually… I'm a "Wartime President.""



The high price Americans will pay for the "Big Lie" is terrifying. "This was a fraudulent election, and the election was stolen."

Steve Bannon, former Trump's adviser, was caught on audio saying Trump is going to lie if he loses the election no matter what, he's going to lie. The video is from a few days before the 2020 presidential election.

https://twitter.com/MisterSalesman/status/15479990568776663313

During a Press Conference

Reporter: Win, lose, or draw in this election will you commit here today for a peaceful transfer of power. There has been rioting on a level in many cities across the country in the street in your so called red and blue states.

Will you commit to a transfer of power after the election?

Trump: Well, we're going to have to see what happens you know that I've been complaining very strongly about the ballots and the ballots are disaster and… and .. and get rid of the ballots and you'll a very transfer … will have a peaceful … there won't be a transfer frankly there will be a continuation … the ballots are out of control you know it and you knows who knows better than anybody else the democrats know it better than anybody else.

https://twitter.com/MisterSalesman/status/1376113940116217857

# Dead People

"Dead People voted. We Won Big!"

"I hated it, Kelly, when we got ballots in from the military, with Trump all over it, and they got thrown into a river.

You saw that: they threw ballots into a river from the military, with my name..."

"Dead people,"

Trump said. "So dead people voted, and I think the number is close to 5,000 people. And they went to obituaries. They went to all sorts of methods to come up with an accurate number, and a minimum is close to about 5,000 voters."

He also claimed that "a tremendous number of dead people" voted in Michigan, adding:

"I think it was … 18,000. Some unbelievably high number, much higher than yours, you were in the 4-5,000 category."

"upward of 5,000" dead voters he said was presented to Georgia officials, Raffensperger, said: "The actual number were two. Two. Two people that were dead that voted. So that's wrong."

Trump insisted: "In one state, we have a tremendous amount of dead people. So I don't know – I'm sure we do in Georgia, too. I'm sure we do in Georgia, too." Mark Meadows, told Raffensperger: "You say they were only two dead people who would vote. I can promise you there are more than that."

Then on Jan 6, Trump incited the crowd and told them to stop the certification of Joe Biden and overthrow the will of the people. He said, "The election was stolen and you better fight like hell or you won't have a country."

~

Trump to news media, "They call them DUMPS big Massive DUMPS,

And what happened if you watched the election

I was called by the biggest people … uh
saying congratulations political people …

congratulations sir you just won the
election it was 10 o'clock and you looked
at the numbers

I'm sure you felt that way this election
was over then they did dumps they call
them dumps big massive dumps uh in
Michigan and Pennsylvania and uh uh all
over uh uh if you take a look at…

https://twitter.com/MisterSalesman/sta
tus/1333193166422466565

# The Devil Says I Don't Want to be Your Friend

*For the wrath of God is revealed from heaven against all ungodliness and unrighteousness of men, who by their unrighteousness suppress the truth. (Romans 1:18)*

Trump threatens Mike Pence, the Vice President, to overthrow the government.

In his book, Peril, Bob Woodward reported what Trump said to Mike Pence the day before the insurrection and on Jan. 6.

"I don't want to be your friend anymore (if you do this follow the law and the Constitution) you betrayed us I made

you, you were nothing, your career is
over if you don't do what I am telling
you to do. and the next day he said I'm
counting on you to do it my way and if
you don't I picked the wrong man 4
years ago."


https://www.youtube.com/watch?v=BL
VzXO7aStc


Kevin McCarthy on a call with GOP
leaders immediately following the Jan 6
attack.


Less than a month later, he tried to cover
up Donald Trump's crimes by defying a
subpoena to testify.

"When they started breaking in to my office, myself and the staff got removed from the office.

In doing so, I made a phone call to the president telling him what…was going on asking him to tell these people to stop, to make a video and go out.

And I was very intense and very loud about it.

We can not just sweep this under the rug. We need to know why it happened, who did it, and people need to be held accountable for it. And I'm committed to making sure that happens."

https://twitter.com/TPM/status/1534874497110708224

https://www.youtube.com/watch?v=RzGvnSBUxMk

# The Devil Went Down to Georgia

"The conscience of a people is their power."


Don't let it be taken away.


You have empathy, compassion, and respect for others.  He does not.

On January 2, 2021, during an hour-long conference call, then-U.S. President Donald Trump pressured Georgia Secretary of State Brad Raffensperger to change the state's vote totals for the 2020 presidential election.

Let's take a listen. "No, no, I don't want to listen."

No, you need to listen!

Meadows: Okay. Alright. Mr. President, everyone is on the line. This is Mark Meadows, the chief of staff. Just so we all are aware.

On the line is secretary of state and two other individuals. Jordan and Mr. Germany with him. You also have the

attorneys that represent the president,
Kurt and Alex and Cleta Mitchell —
who is not the attorney of record but has
been involved — myself and then the
president. So, Mr. President, I'll turn it
over to you.

Click here to listen or keep reading.

https://twitter.com/MisterSalesman/status/1530325929771384832

https://www.youtube.com/watch?v=AW_Bdf_jGaA

Trump: Okay, thank you very much.
Hello Brad and Ryan and everybody.

We appreciate the time and the call.

So we've spent a lot of time on this, and if we could just go over some of the numbers, I think it's pretty clear that we won.

We won very substantially in Georgia.

You even see it by rally size, frankly.

We'd be getting 25-30,000 people a rally, and the competition would get less than 100 people. And it never made sense.

But we have a number of things.

We have at least 2 or 3 — anywhere from 250 to 300,000 ballots were dropped mysteriously into the rolls.

Much of that had to do with Fulton County, which hasn't been checked.

We think that if you check the signatures — a real check of the signatures going back in Fulton County —

You'll find at least a couple of hundred thousand of forged signatures of people who have been forged. And we are quite sure that's going to happen.

Another tremendous number.

We're going to have an accurate number over the next two days with certified accountants.

But an accurate number will be given,
but it's in the 50s of thousands — and
that's people that went to vote and they
were told they can't vote because they've
already been voted for. And it's a very
sad thing.

They walked out complaining.

But the number's large.

We'll have it for you. But it's much more
than the number of 11,779 that's — the
current margin is only 11,779.

Brad, I think you agree with that, right?
That's something I think everyone — at
least that's a number that everyone
agrees on.

But that's the difference in the votes. But we've had hundreds of thousands of ballots that we're able to actually — we'll get you a pretty accurate number.

You don't need much of a number because the number that in theory I lost by, the margin would be 11,779.

But you also have a substantial number of people, thousands and thousands, who went to the voting place on November 3, were told they couldn't vote, were told they couldn't vote because a ballot had been put on their name.

And you know that's very, very, very, very sad.

We had, I believe it's about 4,502 voters who voted but who weren't on the voter registration list, so it's 4,502 who voted, but they weren't on the voter registration roll, which they had to be.

You had 18,325 vacant address voters.

The address was vacant, and they're not allowed to be counted. That's 18,325.

Smaller number — you had 904 who only voted where they had just a P.O. — a post office box number — and they had a post office box number, and that's not allowed.

We had at least 18,000 — that's on tape, we had them counted very painstakingly — 18,000 voters having to do with ….

She's a vote scammer, a professional
vote scammer and hustler …

That was the tape that's been shown all
over the world that makes everybody
look bad, you, me and everybody else.

Where they got — number one they said
very clearly and it's been reported that
they said there was a major water main
break.

Everybody fled the area.

And then they came back … and her
daughter and a few people.

There were no Republican poll watchers.
Actually, there were no Democrat poll

watchers, I guess they were them. But there were no Democrats, either, and there was no law enforcement.

Late in the morning, early in the morning, they went to the table with the black robe and the black shield, and they pulled out the votes.

Those votes were put there a number of hours before — the table was put there — I think it was, Brad, you would know, it was probably eight hours or seven hours before, and then it was stuffed with votes.

They weren't in an official voter box; they were in what looked to be suitcases or trunks, suitcases, but they weren't in voter boxes.

The minimum number it could be
because we watched it, and they watched
it certified in slow motion instant replay
if you can believe it, but slow motion,
and it was magnified many times over,
and the minimum it was 18,000 ballots,
all for Biden.


You had out-of-state voters.


They voted in Georgia, but they were
from out of state, of 4,925.


You had absentee ballots sent to vacant,
they were absentee ballots sent to vacant
addresses.


They had nothing on them about
addresses, that's 2,326.

And you had dropboxes, which is very
bad. You had dropboxes that were
picked up.

We have photographs, and we have
affidavits from many people.

I don't know if you saw the hearings, but
you have dropboxes where the box was
picked up but not delivered for three
days.

So all sorts of things could have
happened to that box, including, you
know, putting in the votes that you
wanted.

So there were many infractions, and the
bottom line is, many, many times the

11,779 margin that they said we lost by
—



we had vast; I mean the state is in
turmoil over this.


And I know you would like to get to the
bottom of it, although I saw you on
television today, and you said that you
found nothing wrong.


I mean, you know, and I didn't lose the
state, Brad.


People have been saying that it was the
highest vote ever.

There was no way. A lot of the political people said that there's no way they beat me. And they beat me.

They beat me in the …

As you know, every single state, we won every state.

We won every statehouse in the country.

We held the Senate, which is shocking to people, although we'll see what happens tomorrow or in a few days.

And we won the House, but we won every single statehouse, and we won Congress, which was supposed to lose 15 seats, and they gained, I think 16 or 17 or something. I think there's a now difference of five.

There was supposed to be a difference substantially more.

But politicians in every state, but politicians in Georgia have given affidavits and are going to that, that there was no way that they beat me in the election, that the people came out, in fact, they were expecting to lose, and then they ended up winning by a lot because of the coattails.

And they said there's no way, that they've done many polls prior to the election, that there was no way that they won.

Ballots were dropped in massive numbers. And we're trying to get to those numbers and we will have them.

They'll take a period of time. Certified.

But they're massive numbers. And far greater than the 11,779.

The other thing, dead people. So dead people voted, and I think the number is close to 5,000 people. And they went to obituaries.

They went to all sorts of methods to come up with an accurate number, and a minimum is close to about 5,000 voters.

The bottom line is, when you add it all up and then you start adding, you know, 300,000 fake ballots.

Then the other thing they said is in Fulton County and other areas.

And this may or may not be true … this just came up this morning, that they are burning their ballots, that they are shredding, shredding ballots and removing equipment.

They're changing the equipment on the Dominion machines and, you know, that's not legal.

And they supposedly shredded I think they said 300 pounds of, 3,000 pounds of ballots.

And that just came to us as a report
today. And it is a very sad situation.

But Brad, if you took the minimum
numbers where many, many times above
the 11,779, and many of those numbers
are certified, or they will be certified, but
they are certified.

And those are numbers that are there,
that exist.

And that beat the margin of loss, they
beat it, I mean, by a lot, and people
should be happy to have an accurate
count instead of an election where
there's turmoil.

I mean there's turmoil in Georgia and
other places.

You're not the only one, I mean, we have other states that I believe will be flipping to us very shortly. And this is something that —

You know, as an example, I think it in Detroit, I think there's a section, a good section of your state actually, which we're not sure so we're not going to report it yet.

But in Detroit, we had, I think it was, 139 percent of the people voted. That's not too good.

In Pennsylvania, they had well over 200,000 more votes than they had people voting. And that doesn't play too well, and the legislature there is, which is

Republican, is extremely activist and angry.

I mean, there were other things also that were almost as bad as that. But they had as an example, in Michigan, a tremendous number of dead people that voted.

I think it was, I think, Mark, it was 18,000. Some unbelievably high number, much higher than yours, you were in the 4-5,000 category.

And that was checked out laboriously by going through, by going through the obituary columns in the newspapers.

So, I guess with all of it being said, Brad, the bottom line, and provisional ballots, again, you know.

You'll have to tell me about the provisional ballots, but we have a lot of people that were complaining that they weren't able to vote because they were already voted for.

These are great people.

And, you know, they were shellshocked.

I don't know if you call that provisional ballots.

In some states, we had a lot of provisional ballot situations where people were given a provisional ballot because when they walked in on November 3 and they were already voted for.

So that's it. I mean, we have many, many times the number of votes necessary to win the state.

And we won the state, and we won it very substantially and easily, and we're getting, we have, much of this is a very certified, far more certified than we need.

But we're getting additional numbers certified, too. And we're getting pictures of dropboxes being delivered and delivered late.

Delivered three days later, in some cases, plus we have many affidavits to that effect.

Election results under attack: Here are the facts

Meadows: So, Mr. President, if I might be able to jump in, and I'll give Brad a chance.

Mr. Secretary, obviously there is, there are allegations where we believe that not every vote or fair vote and legal vote was counted, and that's at odds with the representation from the secretary of state's office.

What I'm hopeful for is there some way that we can, we can find some kind of agreement to look at this a little bit more fully? You know the president mentioned Fulton County.

But in some of these areas where there seems to be a difference of where the facts seem to lead, and so Mr. Secretary, I was hopeful that, you know, in the spirit of cooperation and compromise, is there something that we can at least have a discussion to look at some of these allegations to find a path forward that's less litigious?

Raffensperger: Well, I listened to what the president has just said. President Trump, we've had several lawsuits, and we've had to respond in court to the lawsuits and the contentions.

We don't agree that you have won. And
we don't

 I didn't agree about the 200,000 number
that you'd mentioned. I'll go through
that point by point.

What we have done is we gave our state
Senate about one and a half hours of our
time going through the election issue by
issue and then on the state House, the
government affairs committee, we gave
them about two and a half hours of our
time, going back point by point on all
the issues of contention.

And then just a few days ago, we met
with our U.S. congressmen, Republican
congressmen, and we gave them about

two hours of our time talking about this past election.

Going back, primarily what you've talked about here focused in on primarily, I believe, is the absentee ballot process. I don't believe that you're really questioning the Dominion machines.

Because we did a hand re-tally, a 100 percent re-tally of all the ballots, and compared them to what the machines said and came up with virtually the same result.

Then we did the recount, and we got virtually the same result. So I guess we can probably take that off the table.

I don't think there's an issue about that.

Trump: Well, Brad. Not that there's not an issue, because we have a big issue with Dominion in other states and perhaps in yours.

But we haven't felt we needed to go there.

And just to, you know, maybe put a little different spin on what Mark is saying, Mark Meadows, yeah we'd like to go further, but we don't really need to.

We have all the votes we need.

You know, we won the state.

If you took, these are the most minimal numbers, the numbers that I gave you, those are numbers that are certified, your absentee ballots sent to vacant addresses, your out-of-state voters, 4,925.

You know when you add them up, it's many more times, it's many times the 11,779 number.

So we could go through, we have not gone through your Dominion.

So we can't give them blessing. I mean, in other states, we think we found tremendous corruption with Dominion machines, but we'll have to see.

But we only lost the state by that number, 11,000 votes, and 779.

So with that being said, with just what we have, with just what we have, we're giving you minimal, minimal numbers.

We're doing the most conservative numbers possible; we're many times, many, many times above the margin. And so we don't really have to, Mark, I don't think we have to go through …

Meadows: Right

Trump: Because what's the difference between winning the election by two votes and winning it by half a million votes.

I think I probably did win it by half a million.

You know, one of the things that happened, Brad, is we have other people coming in now from Alabama and from South Carolina and from other states, and they're saying it's impossible for you to have lost Georgia.

We won.

You know in Alabama, we set a record, got the highest vote ever.

In Georgia, we set a record with a massive amount of votes. And they say it's not possible to have lost Georgia.

And I could tell you by our rallies. I could tell you by the rally I'm having on Monday night, the place, they already have lines of people standing out front waiting.

It's just not possible to have lost Georgia. It's not possible.

When I heard it was close, I said there's no way. But they dropped a lot of votes in there late at night. You know that, Brad. And that's what we are working on very, very stringently.

But regardless of those votes, with all of it being said, we lost by essentially 11,000 votes, and we have many more votes already calculated and certified, too.

And so I just don't know, you know, Mark, I don't know what's the purpose.

I won't give Dominion a pass because we found too many bad things. But we don't need Dominion or anything else.

We have won this election in Georgia based on all of this. And there's nothing wrong with saying that, Brad.

You know, I mean, having the correct — the people of Georgia are angry. And these numbers are going to be repeated on Monday night.

Along with others that we're going to have by that time, which are much more substantial even.

And the people of Georgia are angry, the people of the country are angry.

And there's nothing wrong with saying that, you know, that you've recalculated.

Because the 2,236 in absentee ballots.

I mean, they're all exact numbers that were done by accounting firms, law firms, etc.

And even if you cut 'em in half, cut 'em in half and cut 'em in half again, it's more votes than we need.

Raffensperger: Well, Mr. President, the challenge that you have is the data you have is wrong. We talked to the congressmen, and they were surprised.

But they — I guess there was a person named Mr. Braynard who came to these meetings and presented data, and he said that there was dead people, I believe it was upward of 5,000.

The actual number were two. Two.

Two people that were dead that voted. So that's wrong.

Trump: Well, Cleta, how do you respond to that? Maybe you tell me?

Mitchell: Well, I would say, Mr. Secretary, one of the things that we have requested and what we said was, if you look, if you read our petition, it said that we took the names and birth years, and

we had certain information available to
us.


We have asked from your office for
records that only you have, and so we
said there is a universe of people who
have the same name and same birth year
and died.


But we don't have the records that you
have.


And one of the things that we have been
suggesting formally and informally for
weeks now is for you to make available
to us the records that would be necessary
—

Cleta Mitchell, a key figure in president's phone call, was an early backer of Trump's election fraud claims

Trump: But, Cleta, even before you do that, and not even including that, that's why I hardly even included that number, although in one state, we have a tremendous amount of dead people.

So I don't know — I'm sure we do in Georgia, too. I'm sure we do in Georgia, too.

But we're so far ahead. We're so far ahead of these numbers, even the phony ballots of …, known scammer.

You know the Internet?

You know what was trending on the Internet?

"Where's …?"

Because they thought she'd be in jail. "Where's …?" It's crazy, it's crazy. That was.

The minimum number is 18,000 for … but they think it's probably about 56,000, but the minimum number is 18,000 on the … night where she ran back in there when everybody was gone and stuffed, she stuffed the ballot boxes.

Let's face it, Brad, I mean.

They did it in slow motion replay magnified, right? She stuffed the ballot boxes.

They were stuffed like nobody has ever seen them stuffed before.

So there's a term for it when it's a machine instead of a ballot box, but she stuffed the machine.

She stuffed the ballot. Each ballot went three times, they were showing: Here's ballot No 1. Here it is a second time, third time, next ballot.

I mean, look. Brad. We have a new tape that we're going to release. It's devastating. And by the way, that one event, that one event is much more than the 11,000 votes that we're talking about.

It's, you know, that one event was a disaster. And it's just, you know, but it was, it was something, it can't be disputed.

And again, we have a version that you haven't seen, but it's magnified.

It's magnified, and you can see everything.

For some reason, they put it in three times, each ballot, and I don't know why.

I don't know why three times. Why not five times, right? Go ahead.

Raffensperger: You're talking about the State Farm video. And I think it's extremely unfortunate that Rudy Giuliani or his people, they sliced and diced that video and took it out of context.

The next day, we brought in WSB-TV, and we let them show, see the full run of tape, and what you'll see, the events that transpired are nowhere near what was projected by, you know —

Trump: But where were the poll watchers, Brad?

There were no poll watchers there. There were no Democrats or Republicans.

There was no security there.

It was late in the evening, late in the, early in the morning, and there was nobody else in the room.

Where were the poll watchers, and why did they say a water main broke, which they did and which was reported in the newspapers?

They said they left.

They ran out because of a water main break, and there was no water main.

There was nothing. There was no break.

There was no water main break.

But we're, if you take out everything, where were the Republican poll watchers, even where were the Democrat poll watchers, because there were none.

And then you say, well, they left their station, you know, if you look at the tape, and this was, this was reviewed by professional police and detectives and other people, when they left in a rush, everybody left in a rush because of the water main, but everybody left in a rush.

These people left their station.

When they came back, they didn't go to their station.

They went to the apron, wrapped around the table, under which were thousands and thousands of ballots in a box that was not an official or a sealed box. And then they took those.

They went back to a different station.

So, if they would have come back, they would have walked to their station, and they would have continued to work.

But they couldn't do even that because that's illegal, because they had no Republican poll watchers.

And remember, her reputation is — she's known all over the Internet, Brad. She's known all over.

I'm telling you, "Where's … " was one
of the hot items …

They knew her. "Where's …?"

So Brad, there can be no justification for
that. And I, you know, I give everybody
the benefit of the doubt.

But that was — and Brad, why did they
put the votes in three times? You know,
they put 'em in three times.

Raffensperger: Mr. President, they did
not put that. We did an audit of that, and
we proved conclusively that they were
not scanned three times.

Trump:  Where was everybody else at that late time in the morning?

Where was everybody? Where were the Republicans?

Where were the security guards? Were the people that were there just a little while before when everyone ran out of the room.

How come we had no security in the room.

Why did they run to the bottom of the table?

Why do they run there and just open the skirt and rip out the votes? I mean, Brad.

And they were sitting there, I think for five hours or something like that, the votes.

Raffensperger: Mr. President, we'll send you the link from WSB.

Trump: I don't care about the link. I don't need it. Brad, I have a much better

—

Mitchell: I will tell you. I've seen the tape. The full tape. So has Alex. We've watched it. And what we saw and what we've confirmed in the timing is that they made everybody leave — we have sworn affidavits saying that.

And then they began to process ballots.

And our estimate is that there were roughly 18,000 ballots. We don't know that. If you know that —



Trump: — it was 18,000 ballots, but they used each one three times.



Mitchell: Well, I don't know about that, but I know —



Trump: — well, I do, because we had ours magnified out —



Mitchell: I've watched the entire tape.



Trump: — but nobody can make a case for that, Brad. Nobody. I mean, look, that's, you'd have to be a child to think anything other than that. Just a child. I

mean you have your never-Trumper U.S.
attorney there —

Mitchell: — how many ballots, Mr.
Secretary, are you saying were processed
then?

Raffensperger: We had GBI …
investigate that.

Germany: We had our — this is Ryan
Germany. We had our law enforcement
officers talk to everyone who was, who
was there after that event came to light.
GBI was with them as well as FBI
agents.

Trump: Well, there's no way they could
— then they're incompetent. They're
either dishonest or incompetent, okay?

Mitchell: Well, what did they find?

Trump: There's only two answers, dishonesty or incompetence. There's just no way. Look. There's no way. And on the other thing, I said too, there is no way.

I mean, there's no way that these things could have been, you know, you have all these different people that voted, but they don't live in Georgia anymore.

What was that number, Cleta?

That was a pretty good number, too.

Mitchell: The number who have registered out of state after they moved from Georgia. And so they had a date when they moved from Georgia, they registered to vote out of state, and then it's like 4,500, I don't have that number right in front of me.

Trump: And then they came back in, and they voted.

Mitchell: And voted. Yeah.

Trump: I thought that was a large number, though. It was in the 20s.

Germany: We've been going through each of those as well, and those numbers that we got, that Ms. Mitchell was just saying, they're not accurate. Every one we've been through are people that lived in Georgia, moved to a different state,

but then moved back to Georgia
legitimately. And in many cases —

Trump: How may people do that? They
moved out, and then they said, "Ah, to
hell with it, I'll move back."

You know, it doesn't sound like a very
normal … you mean, they moved out,
and what, they missed it so much that
they wanted to move back in? It's crazy.

Germany: They moved back in years
ago. This was not like something just
before the election. So there's something
about that data that, it's just not accurate.

Trump: Well, I don't know, all I know is
that it is certified. And they moved out

of Georgia, and they voted. It didn't say they moved back in, Cleta, did it?

Fact-checking Trump's call to the Georgia secretary of state

Mitchell: No, but I mean, we're looking at the voter registration. Again, if you have additional records, we've been asking for that, but you haven't shared any of that with us.

You just keep saying you investigated the allegations.

Trump: Cleta, a lot of it you don't need to be shared. I mean, to be honest, they should share it. They should share it because you want to get to an honest election.

I won this election by hundreds of thousands of votes. There's no way I lost Georgia.

There's no way. We won by hundreds of thousands of votes.

I'm just going by small numbers, when you add them up, they're many times the 11,000. But I won that state by hundreds of thousands of votes.

Do you think it's possible that they shredded ballots in Fulton County?

Because that's what the rumor is. And also, that Dominion took out machines.

That Dominion is really moving fast to get rid of their, uh, machinery.

Do you know anything about that? Because that's illegal, right?

Germany: This is Ryan Germany. No, Dominion has not moved any machinery out of Fulton County.

Trump: But have they moved the inner parts of the machines and replaced them with other parts?

Germany:  No.

Trump: Are you sure, Ryan?

Germany: I'm sure. I'm sure, Mr. President.

Trump:  What about, what about the ballots. The shredding of the ballots. Have they been shredding ballots?


Germany:  The only investigation that we have into that — they have not been shredding any ballots. There was an issue in Cobb County where they were doing normal office shredding, getting rid of old stuff, and we investigated that. But this stuff from, you know, from you know past elections.


Trump: It doesn't pass the smell test because we hear they're shredding thousands and thousands of ballots, and now what they're saying, "Oh, we're just cleaning up the office." You know.

Raffensperger: Mr. President, the problem you have with social media, they — people can say anything.

Trump: Oh this isn't social media. This is Trump media. It's not social media. It's really not; it's not social media. I don't care about social media. I couldn't care less. Social media is Big Tech. Big Tech is on your side, you know. I don't even know why you have a side because you should want to have an accurate election. And you're a Republican.

Raffensperger: We believe that we do have an accurate election.

Trump: No, no you don't. No, no you don't. You don't have. Not even close.

You're off by hundreds of thousands of votes. And just on the small numbers, you're off on these numbers, and these numbers can't be just — well, why wont? —

Okay. So you sent us into Cobb County for signature verification, right? You sent us into Cobb County, which we didn't want to go into.

And you said it would be open to the public. So we had our experts there, they weren't allowed into the room. But we didn't want Cobb County.

We wanted Fulton County. And you wouldn't give it to us. Now, why aren't we doing signature — and why can't it be open to the public?

And why can't we have professionals do it instead of rank amateurs who will never find anything and don't want to find anything?

They don't want to find; you know they don't want to find anything.

Someday you'll tell me the reason why, because I don't understand your reasoning, but someday you'll tell me the reason why. But why don't you want to find?

Germany: Mr. President, we chose Cobb County

Trump: Why don't you want to find . . . What?

Germany: Sorry, go ahead.

Trump: So why did you do Cobb County?

We didn't even request — we requested Fulton County, not Cobb County.

Go ahead, please. Go ahead.

Germany:  We chose Cobb County because that was the only county where there's been any evidence submitted that the signature verification was not properly done.

Trump: No, but I told you.

We're not, we're not saying that.

Mitchell: We did say that.

Trump: Fulton County. Look. Stacey, in my opinion, Stacey is as dishonest as they come.

She has outplayed you … at everything.

She got you to sign a totally unconstitutional agreement, which is a disastrous agreement.

You can't check signatures. I can't imagine you're allowed to do harvesting, I guess, in that agreement.

That agreement is a disaster for this country. But she got you somehow to sign that thing, and she has outsmarted you at every step.

And I hate to imagine what's going to happen on Monday or Tuesday, but it's very scary to people.

You know, when the ballots flow in out of nowhere.

It's very scary to people.

That consent decree is a disaster.

It's a disaster. A very good lawyer who examined it said they've never seen anything like it.

Raffensperger: Harvesting is still illegal in the state of Georgia. And that settlement agreement did not change that one iota.

Trump: It's not a settlement agreement, it's a consent decree.

It even says consent decree on it, doesn't it?

It uses the term consent decree. It doesn't say settlement agreement.

It's a consent decree. It's a disaster.

Raffensperger: It's a settlement agreement.

Trump: What's written on top of it?


Raffensperger: Ryan?


Germany: I don't have it in front of me, but it was not entered by the court, it's not a court order.


Trump: But Ryan, it's called a consent decree, is that right? On the paper. Is that right?


Germany: I don't. I don't. I don't believe so, but I don't have it in front of me.


The Trump- Raffensperger call was big news — unless you were following conservative media

Trump: Okay, whatever, it's a disaster.

It's a disaster. Look. Here's the problem.

We can go through signature verification, and we'll find hundreds of thousands of signatures, if you let us do it.

And the only way you can do it, as you know, is to go to the past.

But you didn't do that in Cobb County.

You just looked at one page compared to another.

The only way you can do a signature verification is go from the one that signed it on November whatever.

Recently.

And compare it to two years ago, four years ago, six years ago, you know, or even one. And you'll find that you have many different signatures.

But in Fulton, where they dumped ballots, you will find that you have many that aren't even signed and you have many that are forgeries.

Okay, you know that. You know that. You have no doubt about that.

And you will find you will be at 11,779 within minutes because Fulton County is totally corrupt, and so is she totally corrupt.

And they're going around playing you and laughing at you behind your back, Brad, whether you know it or not, they're laughing at you.

And you've taken a state that's a Republican state, and you've made it almost impossible for a Republican to win because of cheating, because they cheated like nobody's ever cheated before.

And I don't care how long it takes me, you know, we're going to have other states coming forward — pretty good.

But I won't … this is never … this is …

We have some incredible talent said
they've never seen anything …

Now the problem is they need more
time for the big numbers.

But they're very substantial numbers. But
I think you're going to find that they —
by the way, a little information —

I think you're going to find that they are
shredding ballots because they have to
get rid of the ballots because the ballots
are unsigned.

The ballots are corrupt, and they're
brand new, and they don't have seals,

and there's a whole thing with the
ballots.

But the ballots are corrupt.

And you are going to find that they are
— which is totally illegal — it is more
illegal for you than it is for them because,
you know, what they did and you're not
reporting it.

That's a criminal, that's a criminal
offense. And you can't let that happen.

That's a big risk to you and to Ryan,
your lawyer. And that's a big risk. But
they are shredding ballots, in my
opinion, based on what I've heard.

And they are removing machinery, and they're moving it as fast as they can, both of which are criminal finds.

And you can't let it happen, and you are letting it happen. You know, I mean, I'm notifying you that you're letting it happen.

So look. All I want to do is this. I just want to find 11,780 votes, which is one more than we have because we won the state.

And flipping the state is a great testament to our country because, you know, this is — it's a testament that they can admit to a mistake or whatever you want to call it.

If it was a mistake, I don't know.

A lot of people think it wasn't a mistake. It was much more criminal than that.

But it's a big problem in Georgia, and it's not a problem that's going away. I mean, you know, it's not a problem that's going away.

Germany: This is Ryan. We're looking into every one of those things that you mentioned.

Trump: Good. But if you find it, you've got to say it, Ryan.

Germany: Let me tell you what we are seeing. What we're seeing is not at all what you're describing.

These are investigators from our office, these are investigators from GBI, and they're looking, and they're good.

And that's not what they're seeing. And we'll keep looking, at all these things.

Trump: Well, you better check on the ballots because they are shredding ballots, Ryan. I'm just telling you, Ryan.

They're shredding ballots. And you should look at that very carefully.

Because that's so illegal. You know, you may not even believe it because it's so bad.

But they're shredding ballots because they think we're going to eventually get there …

 because we'll eventually get into Fulton. In my opinion, it's never too late. … So, that's the story.

Look, we need only 11,000 votes. We have are far more than that as it stands now. We'll have more and more.

And … do you have provisional ballots at all, Brad? Provisional ballots?

Raffensperger: Provisional ballots are allowed by state law.

Trump: Sure, but I mean, are they counted, or did you just hold them back because they, you know, in other words, how many provisional ballots do you have in the state?

Raffensperger: We'll get you that number.

Trump: Because most of them are made out to the name Trump. Because these are people that were scammed when they came in.

And we have thousands of people that have testified or that want to testify.

When they came in, they were proudly
going to vote on November 3.


And they were told, "I'm sorry, you've
already been voted for, you've already
voted."


The women, men started screaming,
"No. I proudly voted till November 3."


They said, "I'm sorry, but you've already
been voted for, and you have a ballot."
And these people are beside themselves.


So, they went out, and they filled in a
provisional ballot, putting the name
Trump on it.

And what about that batch of military ballots that came in. And even though I won the military by a lot, it was 100 percent Trump. I mean 100 percent Biden.

Do you know about that? A large group of ballots came in, I think it was to Fulton County, and they just happened to be 100 percent for Trump — for Biden — even though Trump won the military by a lot, you know, a tremendous amount. But these ballots were 100 percent for Biden. And do you know about that?

A very substantial number came in, all for Biden.

Does anybody know about it?

Mitchell: I know about it, but —

Trump: Okay, Cleta, I'm not asking you, Cleta, honestly. I'm asking Brad.

Do you know about the military ballots that we have confirmed now.

Do you know about the military ballots that came in that were 100 percent, I mean 100 percent, for Biden. Do you know about that?

Germany:  I don't know about that. I do know that we have, when military ballots come in, it's not just military, it's also military and overseas citizens.

The military part of that does generally go Republican.

The overseas citizen part of it generally goes very Democrat. This was a mix of 'em.

Trump: No, but this was. That's okay. But I got like 78 percent of the military.

These ballots were all for …

They didn't tell me overseas. Could be overseas, too, but I get votes overseas, too, Ryan, in all fairness.

No they came in, a large batch came in, and it was, quote, 100 percent for Biden. And that is criminal. You know, that's criminal.

Okay. That's another criminal, that's another of the many criminal events, many criminal events here.

I don't know, look, Brad. I got to get …

I have to find 12,000 votes, and I have them times a lot. And therefore, I won the state.

That's before we go to the next step, which is in the process of right now.

You know, and I watched you this morning, and you said, well, there was no criminality.

But I mean all of this stuff is very dangerous stuff.

When you talk about no criminality, I think it's very dangerous for you to say that.

I just, I just don't know why you don't want to have the votes counted as they are.

Like even you when you went and did that check. And I was surprised because, you know …

And we found a few thousand votes that were against me.

I was actually surprised because the way that check was done, all you're doing, you know, recertifying existing votes and, you know, and you were given votes and you just counted them up, and you still found 3,000 that were bad.

So that was sort of surprising that it came down to three or five, I don't know.

Still a lot of votes. But you have to go back to check from past years with respect to signatures.

And if you check with Fulton County, you'll have hundreds of thousands because they dumped ballots into Fulton County and the other county next to it.

So, what are we going to do here, folks? I only need 11,000 votes. Fellas, I need 11,000 votes. Give me a break.

You know, we have that in spades already.

Or we can keep it going, but that's not fair to the voters of Georgia because they're going to see what happened, and they're going to see what happened.

I mean, I'll, I'll take on anybody you want with regard to … and her lovely daughter, a very lovely young lady, I'm sure. But, but …

I will take on anybody you want. And the minimum, there were 18,000 ballots, but they used them three times.

So that's, you know, a lot of votes.

And they were all to Biden, by the way, that's the other thing we didn't say.

You know, …. the one thing I forgot to say, which was the most important.

You know that every single ballot she did went to Biden. You know that, right?

Do you know that, by the way, Brad?

Every single ballot that she did through the machines at early, early in the morning went to Biden.

Did you know that, Ryan?

Germany: That's not accurate, Mr. President.

Trump: Huh. What is accurate?

Germany: The numbers that we are showing are accurate.

Trump: No, about ... About early in the morning, Ryan.

Where the woman took, you know, when the whole gang took the stuff from under the table, right?

Do you know, do you know who those ballots, do you know who they were made out to, do you know who they were voting for?

Germany: No, not specifically.

Trump: Did you ever check?

Germany: We did what I described to you earlier.

Trump: No no no — did you ever check the ballots that were scanned by … a known political operative, balloter? Did ever check who those votes were for?

Germany: We looked into that situation that you described.

Trump: No, they were 100 percent for Biden. 100 percent. There wasn't a Trump vote in the whole group.

Why don't you want to find this, Ryan? What's wrong with you? I heard your lawyer is very difficult, actually, but I'm sure you're a good lawyer.

You have a nice last name.

But, but I'm just curious, why wouldn't, why do you keep fighting this thing? It just doesn't make sense.

We're way over the 17,779, right?

We're way over that number, and just if you took just … we're over that number by five, five or six times when you multiply that times three.

And every single ballot went to Biden, and you didn't know that, but now you know it.

So, tell me, Brad, what are we going to do?

We won the election, and it's not fair to take it away from us like this. And it's going to be very costly in many ways.

And I think you have to say that you're going to reexamine it, and you can reexamine it, but reexamine it with people that want to find answers, not people that don't want to find answers.

For instance, I'm hearing Ryan that he's probably, I'm sure a great lawyer and everything, but he's making statements about those ballots that he doesn't know.

But he's making them with such — he did make them with surety.

But now I think he's less sure because the answer is, they all went to Biden, and that alone wins us the election by a lot.

You know, so.

Raffensperger: Mr. President, you have people that submit information, and we have our people that submit information.

And then it comes before the court, and the court then has to make a determination.

We have to stand by our numbers. We believe our numbers are right.

Trump: Why do you say that, though? I don't know. I mean, sure, we can play this game with the courts, but why do you say that?

First of all, they don't even assign us a judge. They don't even assign us a judge.

But why wouldn't you … Hey Brad, why wouldn't you want to check out?

And why wouldn't you want to say, hey, if in fact, President Trump is right about that, then he wins the state of Georgia, just that one incident alone without going through hundreds of thousands of dropped ballots.

You just say, you stick by, I mean I've been watching you, you know, you don't care about anything.

 "Your numbers are right." But your numbers aren't right.

They're really wrong, and they're really wrong, Brad.

And I know this phone call is going nowhere other than, other than ultimately, you know —

Look, ultimately, I win, okay?

Because you guys are so wrong. And you treated this.

You treated the population of Georgia
so badly.

You, between you and your governor,
who is down at 21, he was down 21
points.

And like a schmuck, I endorsed him, and
he got elected, but I will tell you, he is a
disaster.

The people are so angry in Georgia, I
can't imagine he's ever getting elected
again, I'll tell you that much right now.

But why wouldn't you want to find the
right answer, Brad, instead of keep
saying that the numbers are right? 'Cause
those numbers are so wrong?

Mitchell: Mr. Secretary, Mr. President, one of the things that we have been, Alex can talk about this, we talked about it, and I don't know whether the information has been conveyed to your office, but I think what the president is saying, and what we've been trying to do is to say, look, the court is not acting on our petition.

They haven't even assigned a judge.

But the people of Georgia and the people of America have a right to know the answers. And you have data and records that we don't have access to.

And you can keep telling us and making public statement that you investigated this and nothing to see here.

But we don't know about that. All we know is what you tell us.

What I don't understand is why wouldn't it be in everyone's best interest to try to get to the bottom, compare the numbers, you know, if you say, because … to try to be able to get to the truth because we don't have any way of confirming what you're telling us.

You tell us that you had an investigation at the State Farm Arena. I don't have any report.

I've never seen a report of investigation. I don't know that is. I've been pretty involved in this, and I don't know.

And that's just one of 25 categories. And it doesn't even. And as I, as the president said, we haven't even gotten into the Dominion issue.

That's not part of our case.

It's not part of, we just didn't feel as though we had any to be able to develop —

Trump: No, we do have a way, but I don't want to get into it. We found a way … excuse me, but we don't need it because we're only down 11,000 votes, so we don't even need it.

I personally think they're corrupt as hell. But we don't need that.

All we have to do, Cleta, is find 11,000-plus votes. So we don't need that.

I'm not looking to shake up the whole world. We won Georgia easily.

We won it by hundreds of thousands of votes.

But if you go by basic, simple numbers, we won it easily, easily.

So, we're not giving Dominion a pass on the record.

We don't need Dominion because we have so many other votes that we don't need to prove it any more than we already have.

Hilbert: Mr. President and Cleta, this is Kurt Hilbert, if I might interject for a moment.

Ryan, I would like to suggest that just four categories that have already been mentioned by the president that have actually hard numbers of 24,149 votes that were counted illegally.

That in and of itself is sufficient to change the results or place the outcome in doubt.

We would like to sit down with your office, and we can do it through purposes of compromise and just like this phone call, just to deal with that limited category of votes.

And if you are able to establish that our numbers are not accurate, then fine.

However, we believe that they are accurate.

We've had now three to four separate experts looking at these numbers.

Trump: Certified accountants looked at them.

Hilbert: Correct. And this is just based on USPS data and your own secretary of state data.

So that's what we would entreat and ask you to do, to sit down with us in a compromise and settlements proceeding and actually go through the registered voter IDs and the registrations.

And if you can convince us that 24,149 is inaccurate, then fine.

But we tend to believe that is, you know, obviously more than 11,779. That's sufficient to change the results entirely in and of itself. So what would you say to that, Mr. Germany?

Germany: I'm happy to get with our lawyers, and we'll set that up. That number is not accurate. And I think we can show you, for all the ones we've looked at, why it's not.

And so if that would be helpful, I'm happy to get with our lawyers and set that up with you guys.

Trump: Well, let me ask you, Kurt, you think that is an accurate number. That was based on the information given to you by the secretary of state's department, right?

Hilbert: That is correct. That information is the minimum, most conservative data based upon the USPS data and the secretary of state's office data that has been made publicly available.

We do not have the internal numbers from the secretary of state. Yet we have asked for it six times. I sent a letter over to … several times requesting this information, and it's been rebuffed every single time.

So, it stands to reason that if the information is not forthcoming, there's something to hide. That's the problem that we have.

Germany: Well, that's not the case, sir. There are things that you guys are entitled to get. And there's things that under law, we are not allowed to give out.

Trump: Well, you have to. Well, under law, you're not allowed to give faulty election results, okay? You're not allowed to do that.

And that's what you done.

This is a faulty election result. And honestly, this should go very fast.

You should meet tomorrow because you have a big election coming up, and because of what you've done to the president —

you know, the people of Georgia know that this was a scam — and because of what you've done to the president, a lot of people aren't going out to vote.

And a lot of Republicans are going to vote negative because they hate what you did to the president. Okay? They hate it.

And they're going to vote. And you would be respected. Really respected, if this thing could be straightened out before the election.

You have a big election coming up on Tuesday. And I think that it is really is important that you meet tomorrow and work out on these numbers.

Because I know, Brad, that if you think we're right, I think you're going to say, and I'm not looking to blame anybody, I'm just saying, you know, and, you know, under new counts, and under new views, of the election results, we won the election.

You know? It's very simple.

We won the election. As the governors of major states and the surrounding states said, there is no way you lost Georgia.

As the Georgia politicians say, there is no way you lost Georgia. Nobody. Everyone knows I won it by hundreds of thousands of votes.

But I'll tell you it's going to have a big impact on Tuesday if you guys don't get this thing straightened out fast.

Meadows: Mr. President, this is Mark.

It sounds like we've got two different sides agreeing that we can look at those areas, and I assume that we can do that within the next 24 to 48 hours, to go ahead and get that reconciled so that we can look at the two claims and making sure that we get the access to the secretary of state's data to either validate or invalidate the claims that have been made.

Is that correct?

Germany: No, that's not what I said. I'm happy to have our lawyers sit down with Kurt and the lawyers on that side and explain to him, hey, here's, based on what we've looked at so far, here's how

we know this is wrong, this is wrong, this
is wrong, this is wrong, this is wrong.

Meadows: So what you're saying, Ryan,
let me let me make sure … so what
you're saying is you really don't want to
give access to the data. You just want to
make another case on why the lawsuit is
wrong?

Germany: I don't think we can give
access to data that's protected by law.
But we can sit down with them and say
—

Trump: But you're allowed to have a
phony election? You're allowed to have a
phony election, right?

Germany: No, sir.

Trump: When are you going to do signature counts, when are you going to do signature verification on Fulton County, which you said you were going to do, and now all of a sudden, you're not doing it.

When are you doing that?

Germany: We are going to do that. We've announced —

Hilbert: To get to this issue of the personal information and privacy issue, is it possible that the secretary of state could deputize the lawyers for the president so that we could access that information and private information without you having any kind of violation?

Trump: Well, I don't want to know who it is. You guys can do it very confidentially. You can sign a confidentiality agreement.

That's okay. I don't need to know names.

But on this stuff that we're talking about, we got all that information from the secretary of state.

Meadows: Yeah. So let me let me recommend, Ryan, if you and Kurt will get together, you know, when we get off of this phone call, if you could get together and work out a plan to address some of what we've got with your attorneys where we can we can actually look at the data.

For example, Mr. Secretary, I can you say
they were only two dead people who
would vote.

I can promise you there are more than
that. And that may be what your
investigation shows, but I can promise
you there are more than that.

But at the same time, I think it's
important that we go ahead and move
expeditiously to try to do this and
resolve it as quickly as we possibly can.
And if that's the good next step.

Hopefully we can, we can finish this
phone call and go ahead and agree that
the two of you will get together
immediately.

Trump: Well, why don't my lawyers
show you where you got the
information. It will show the secretary of
state, and you don't even have to look at
any names.

We don't want names.

We don't care. But we got that
information from you.

And Stacey Abrams is laughing about
you.

She's going around saying these guys are
dumber than a rock.

What she's done to this party is unbelievable, I tell you. And I only ran against her once.

And that was with a guy named Brian Kemp, and I beat her. And if I didn't run, Brian wouldn't have had even a shot, either in the general or in the primary.

He was dead, dead as a doornail. He never thought he had a shot at either one of them.

What a schmuck I was. But that's the way it is. That's the way it is. I would like you … for the attorneys …

I'd like you to perhaps meet with Ryan, ideally tomorrow, because I think we

should come to a resolution of this
before the election.

Otherwise, you're going to have people
just not voting. They don't want to vote.

They hate the state, they hate the
governor, and they hate the secretary of
state. I will tell you that right now.

The only people that like you are people
that will never vote for you. You know
that, Brad, right?

They like you, you know, they like you.
They can't believe what they found.

They want more people like you. So,
look, can you get together tomorrow?

And, Brad, we just want the truth. It's
simple.

And everyone's going to look very good
if the truth comes out.

It's okay. It takes a little while, but let the
truth come out. And the real truth is, I
won by 400,000 votes.

At least. That's the real truth. But we
don't need 400,000 votes.

We need less than 2,000 votes. And are
you guys able to meet tomorrow, Ryan?

Germany: I'll get with Chris, the lawyer
who's representing us in the case, and
see when he can get together with Kurt.

Raffensperger: Ryan will be in touch
with the other attorney on this call, Mr.
Meadows. Thank you, President Trump,
for your time.


Trump: Okay, thank you, Brad. Thank
you, Ryan.


Thank you. Thank you, everybody.
Thank you very much.


Bye.

# PAUSE

For the love of your country, your faith, mom's apple pie, democracy, dogs, cats, and everything else that is decent and right and good.  Please stay (woke) and don't go back to sleep.

We're going to take a deep dive into the past and see how evil has been brewing in America for years.

* PC users hold down the control to click on resource links.

# Common Sense & The Veil of Secrecy

*Man shoots a squirrel,*

*climbs a tree and shoots a deer,*

*hunts lions for game, tigers & crocodiles*
*for skins, elephants for tusks.*

*Man went to Africa and*
*brought other men in chains*

*on ships and made them slaves*
*to make him rich;*

*Man is evil … lives in wickedness.*

Who were the men behind the writing of the Constitution? It was never about freedom and justice for all; instead, it was designed to create a system that would benefit white privilege. Thomas Jefferson, George Washington, and some other framers were wealthy slave owners.

Whom does the Constitution protect?

Who were the framers afraid of ruling the country?

I often wonder what it would be like to witness the formation of the Constitution and hear the unfiltered thoughts of the framers, including George Washington, James Madison,

Thomas Jefferson, and Benjamin
Franklin.

But then I remember the private letters
they exchanged, letters that may hold the
answers I seek.

It makes me question whether this is real
life because what's happening today is
just a reflection of what occurred in the
past.

The letters written by the framers of the
Constitution are deeply relevant,
disturbing, and powerful beyond what
we can fully comprehend.

They were coded and intended to be
kept hidden behind a veil of secrecy,
never meant to be seen by the public eye.

The fact that they were kept hidden for so long only adds to their significance.

## Records of the Federal Convention of 1787

"To argue with a man who has renounced the use and authority of reason and whose philosophy consists in holding humanity in contempt is like administering medicine to the dead or endeavoring to convert an atheist by scripture." To General Sir William Howe Thomas Paine: Common Sense

Profound words, one observer said. Profoundly important, another tweeted. But this is how it is, and how it was, and how it will always be.

Years ago, I read a quote from
Global&Mail, "You're looking for
people who are equal parts intelligence
and stupidity who possess a clear view of
reality as well as the ability to ignore
reality." Or may I say it this way, "You're
looking for people that are just plain
stupid that believe anything that you tell
them and loyalty over intelligence?

If you put your trust in one man above
all else, disregarding the advice of
scientific experts, medical professionals,
news outlets, and government agencies,
and neglecting your own common sense
and personal well-being, then you have
been fully indoctrinated into a cult.

Those who do not learn from history are
destined to repeat its mistakes.

"History may distort truth and will distort it for a time, by the superior efforts of justification of those who are conscious of needing it most.

Nor will the opening scenes of our present government be seen in their true aspect until letters of the day, now held in private hoards, shall be broken up and laid in private view.

What a treasure will be found in Washington's cabinet when it shall pass into the hands of as candid a friend to truth as he was himself!"

[Thomas Jefferson to Justice William Johnson, June 12, 1823, Letters found online MHI: Adam's Papers.] This letter addresses over 700 ciphered letters (coded) which is what has kept them private from academic scrutiny.

The Framers of the Constitution, what were they afraid of? They were worried about the idea of part of the government taking too much power. They were worried the executive might become a monarch.

On the other hand, they feared that the majority could trample on the rights of a minority, in this case, the wealthy.

They knew one-day things would fall apart. Benjamin Franklin said on the closing day of the convention in 1787: "I agree to this Constitution with all its faults if they are such…."

"We have a Republic if we can keep it."

Fast Forward: 1972-2021

Richard Nixon, Watergate Coverup

Donald Trump, The Big Lie

Jan 6 Attack on the Capitol

Jan 6 Commission Investigates

Trump filed a lawsuit to prevent 700 documents from being turned over and prevent enforcement of lawful subpoenas. A baseless claim of executive privilege to cover his attempt to overthrow the government.

At least 250 new laws have been proposed in 43 states to limit mail, early in-person, and Election Day voting.

President Donald J. Trump has requested the Supreme Court to block the release of his White House records to the January 6 committee.

He argued that "There will not be another Presidential transition for more than three years; Congress has time to allow this Court to consider this expedited appeal." Notably, he did not mention that Republicans could terminate the Jan 6 investigation if they win the 2022 election and establish committees that include individuals who participated in the insurrection.

**The Veil of Secrecy**

Rewind: The year, 1821. The attempt to prevent letters of the Convention from being turned over to the viewing public. (Coded letters)

Montpeler, Sept 15, 1821

To Thomas Richie

(Confidential)

Dear Sir,

I have recd. yours of 8th instant on the subject of the proceedings of the convention of 1787.

It is true that the public has been led to understand that I possess materials for a pretty ample view of what passed in the Assembly.

It is also true that it has not been my intention that they should for ever remain under the veil of secrecy of the time when it might be improper for them to see the light. I had formed no particular determination.

In general, it had appeared to me that it might be best to let the work to be a posthumous one, or at least that its publication should be delayed till the Constitution should be well settled by practice, & till a knowledge of the controversial part of proceedings of its framers could be turned to no improper account.

Delicacy also seemed to require some respect to the rule by the Constitution "prohibited a promulgation without leave of what was spoken in it;" so long as the policy of that rule could be regarded as in any degree expired.

As a guide in expounding and applying the provisions of the Constitution, the debates and incidental decisions of the Convention can have no authoritative character.

However, desirable it be that they should be preserved as gratification to the laudable curiosity felt by every people to trace the origin and progress of their political institutions, & as a source perhaps of some lights as the Science of Govt. the legitimate meaning of the instrument must be derived from the text itself; or if a key is sought to be elsewhere, it must be not in the opinions or intentions of the Body which planned & proposed the Constitution, but in the sense attached to it by the people in their respective State Conventions where it recd. all the authority which it possesses.

Such being the course of my reflections I have suffered a concurrence & continuance of particular inconveniences for the time past, to prevent me from giving to my notes the fair and full preparation due to the subject of them.

[James Madison Records of the Federal Convention of 1787.]

"Never be deceived that the rich will allow you to vote away their wealth."
Lucy Parsons

The rich constituted a minority, and the framers of the Constitution feared that the majority might infringe upon their rights. It may be difficult to believe, but what if you were wealthy and had the power to take over a country?

Would you draft laws to favor the affluent and ensure that people of color, the poor, and working-class whites never governed the land? Laws veiled in secrecy to subdue the majority? Of course not, would you?

How can there be equality when the rich have more money to hire lobbyists, donate more money to political candidates, and persuade lawmakers to craft laws that appear to serve the people but are actually designed to benefit themselves?

 Trump's 2023 campaign speech to wealthy donors: "You're all people that have a lot of money. I know … that you're rich as hell. We're gonna give you tax cuts. We're going to do all the things that we have to." The MAGA crowd laughs. One fella yells, "Yeah, you're our man, Trump."

"Hey, but I'm not rich. What about me? What about the poor people? What are you going to do for them?"

They are willing to sacrifice human lives for the sake of money and power. The word "evil" doesn't even begin to describe it.

Thomas Jefferson wrote, "All men are created equal." (But not the slaves; they were considered to be property), and Jefferson, the 3rd President of the United States owned more than 600 slaves in his lifetime. Imagine that.

https://whitehousehistory.org/slavery-in-the-thomas-jefferson-white-house

# What To the Slave Is the Fourth of July

On the 4th of July, 1852, Fredrick Douglass, a former slave, was invited by the citizens of Rochester, New York, to give a speech as part of their 4th of July celebration.

"This certainly sounds large and out of the common way for me. It's true that I have often had the privilege to speak in this beautiful hall ... the fact is the distance between this platform & the slave plantation for which I escaped is considerable..."

Listen to the 4th of July Speech

https://www.youtube.com/watch?v=H-cVwuMmylA&list=RDH-cVwuMmylA&start_radio=1&t=0


## The Story of Fredrick Douglass


https://www.youtube.com/watch?v=qWcbqlSTYeg

# You're Probably Wrong About a Lot of Things

They are not the same Republicans that abolished slavery & had the people's interest; it's been a flip flop--they are those Confederates who engaged in Civil War.

The truth about Confederate Monuments.  I dare you to watch it…. Okay, I double dare you.

https://www.youtube.com/watch?v=otTsbqK4U7o&list=PLIdsHKV3qWofxAKbDcU5Somr466hcFk6V&index=25

"You Want a Confederate Monument? My Body Is a Confederate Monument. I have rape-colored skin. My light brown blackness is a living testament to the rules, the practices, causes of the old South..."

Watch the video

https://www.youtube.com/watch?v=vIdiI3m7OMg

Helen Plane, the head of United Daughters of Confederacy (KKK) "I feel it's due to the Klan which saved us from Negro domination & carpetbag rule, that it be immortalized on Stone Mountain. Why not represent a small group of them in their nightly uniform approaching in the distance?"

https://www.kqed.org/lowdown/19119/stone-mountains-hidden-history-americas-biggest-confederate-memorial-and-birthplace-of-the-modern-ku-klux-klan

Reconstruction

https://youtu.be/-k3ioHtk95E?t=831

https://www.youtube.com/watch?v=g5svdBw7J3o&list=PLIdsHKV3qWofxAKbDcU5Somr466hcFk6V&index=12

"The 1619 Project. August 1619: A ship arrives in Point Comfort, a costal port of British Colony of Virginia, carrying between 20-30 enslaved Africans.  They are sold to the colonists in exchange for provisions."

https://www.youtube.com/watch?v=XrfV7w3EyGI

# Why Do We Hate Each Other?

Why do people hate rats?

Is it because they carry diseases?

But what about squirrels? They also have diseases.

Something is wrong with this picture.

We are taught to hate rats, much like we are taught to hate people.

We are not born to hate, nor is it in our genes.

Skin color has nothing to do with a person's intelligence or worth as a human being.

The racist is the true person of color, not black or brown people, but the one whose color turns red with anger and embarrassment, pale when sick or scared, or tan or darker like our brothers whom they hate.

Their ignorance is undignified bliss, with a history hidden by shame. But today, they are shamelessly proud of making graven images, statues, and monuments out of men and calling them heroes for killing and mutilating other men, making people believe they were savages.

For the bigot and the bigots of the world, it makes them feel necessary that they are worth something, but they are sick inside.

Skin color doesn't make you more intelligent or superior to another race. The true people of color in this human race are those who know that we are all Superior!

We are all the same. One blood. One people.

# Am I Next?

"Black people love their children with a kind of obsession. You are all we have, and you come to us endangered." --Ta-Neshisi Coates, Between the World and Me.

Black people know the truth.

They know exactly what's going on.

It's the White people that don't know the Truth.

–Pete Carroll, Seahawks

Police officer Derik Chauvin put his knee on George Floyd's neck for 9/12 minutes, killing him.  George pleaded for his life, "I can't breathe… Momma, Momma" If it weren't for a teenager videoing the incident, Chauvin and the other officers would have gotten away with murder in broad daylight.

https://www.youtube.com/watch?v=FGCFHQ4yfdg

https://www.youtube.com/watch?v=GccRTCDPQmA

AM I Next?

Did you see a card here?

Clerk: What's that?

Man: Card, I left a card here.
Clerk: No.

Man: I'll pay for it.

Cop: Do you have ID Partner?

Man: Yea, I do somewhere around here.

Cop: I need to see it.

Man: You can see whatever I don't care bro.



Why do some people react with "all lives matter" upon hearing the phrase "Black Lives Matter"? The purpose of the BLM slogan is to draw attention to police brutality against Black people and people of color. Responding with "all lives matter" is a method of disregarding and erasing the existence of racial injustice when Black lives are in peril every day.

And some who say "all lives matter" may do so without comprehending or empathizing with the pain and suffering experienced by Black people. These same individuals may also believe that racism does not exist and be quick to declare, "I'm not racist."

Black people cannot begin to heal if people refuse to acknowledge the prevalence of social injustice and racial discrimination and law enforcement officers who have the authority to take lives without consequence.

Consider the possibility that your 18-year-old son went to the store and never came back. He was shot 95 times by a police officer during a traffic stop.

Trump described his joy in watching law enforcement authorities move in on crowds in Minneapolis... during the 2020

Black Lives Matter Protest over George Floyd.

"I don't know, there's something about that—when you watch everybody getting pushed around — there's something very beautiful about it. I don't care what I'm doing." What a fucking psycho!  Sorry, but someone had to say it.

Warning:  Police Brutality

For all the pictures there are millions more!

Police officers ripped a 1-year-old from his mother's arms for sitting on the waiting room floor when there were no chairs.

This is TERRIBLE

Phoenix cops held this black family at gunpoint and threatened to shoot the mother dead because her 4yr old walked out of the store with a doll without her noticing.



A cop pulls a gun on a student picking up trash outside his dorm. Watch how the cop sets the student up to shoot him by saying he feels threatened.

https://twitter.com/MisterSalesman/sta
tus/1387670425992417280


Unequal Justice


Cops have more patience with
Caucasians even when they have a knife
...


https://twitter.com/MisterSalesman/sta
tus/1352782299583164419


Enough is Enough


https://twitter.com/MisterSalesman/sta
tus/1351357272572764166

No need for handcuffs, taser, or backup, and not once did the 2 cops fear for their lives after beating one with his own baton and stealing the police car.

https://twitter.com/MisterSalesman/status/1544032879981862914

Last… but not least. Cops try to capture an alligator in a residential neighborhood. The alligator resisted and knocked out one person with its tail. Not a shot fired. If black, human would be shot ten times.

https://twitter.com/MisterSalesman/status/1569742570074374145

After the jury announced the verdict …


"I just cried so hard," 18 year-old Danelia Frazier  wrote on Facebook. "This last hour my heart was beating so fast, I was so anxious, anxiety bussing through the roof. But to know GUILTY ON 3 CHARGES !!!  THANK YOU GOD THANK YOU THANK YOU THANK YOU.


https://twitter.com/MisterSalesman/status/1385477786790285317

# Systemic Racism

*"Racism is like an alligator,*

*a dinosaur that never went extinct but evolved.*

*--Stamped (Racism, Antiracism, and You)*

Republican Lee Atwater said it was accepted in 1954 for political candidates to say Nigger, nigger, to win votes because they knew their voters were racists. "By 1968, you can't say nigger—backfires. That hurts your chances of winning. So, you say things like forced busing, states' rights, and all the stuff." Racism became coded, a dog whistle.

A reporter asked Malcom X, "Do you feel however like we are making progress in this country…

Malcom X, "No, no, I would never say that progress is being made if you stick a knife in my back 9 inches and pull it out 6 inches there's no progress. If you pull it all the way out that's not progress. The progress is healing the wound that the blow made."

"They haven't even begun to pull the knife out they haven't even tried to pull the knife out ... they won't even admit the knife is there."

https://twitter.com/MisterSalesman/status/1545917290952228866

How Martin Luther King Jr. Changed the World

https://www.youtube.com/watch?v=xabWOU6tU-M

"In order to understand systemic racism, we must educate and visit the past when black men and women were publicly lynched and celebrated by thousands of people."

https://www.youtube.com/watch?v=uHQK1rNd7Qo

## White Rage: The Unspoken Truth of our Nation's Divide

https://www.youtube.com/watch?v=YBYUET24K1c&list=PLIdsHKV3qWofxAKbDcU5Somr466hcFk6V&index=31

## The Tulsa Massacre

https://www.youtube.com/watch?v=ZwptpvcYCvM

"Systemic racism began with the fight for the Senate on February 19,1847. South Carolina Senator John C. Calhoun's speech: Sir, already we are in a minority—Of the 28 States, fourteen are non-slaveholding and fourteen are slaveholding..."

https://teachinghistory.org/history-content/ask-a-historian/23927

# Black Codes

*"Never be deceived that the rich will allow you to vote away their wealth." --Lucy Parsons*

"Hating my people is not the answer we must learn to live together."

YOU mean, learn each other ways & customs. "Yes." And live right next to each other?

"Well, it's a big country."

WHAT happens when generations are born and they forget this is our land.
~Shaka Zulu

You build walls, demean, brainwash, manipulate people, and have the audacity to call yourselves Christian Nationalists. But in reality, your actions are foul. I'm here because your ancestors went to Africa, looted, murdered, raped, and exploited our people taking away our freedom to enrich your  lives through oppression.

Now, you enslave us to a system that makes it harder to vote, get good paying jobs, and quality education, obtain decent housing, impose harsher criminal penalties, and ban books to cover up your crimes. I am the punishment you have brought upon yourselves.

But this time around, it's a different kind of slavery that affects everybody. The system is everywhere.  It is what you learn in school, at home, at church, and what you watch on TV.

The system is on your job; discrimination, low wages, no health insurance.  It affects every aspect of your life, from high rent to high car insurance and credit score.

It's in every government and non-government institution. It's a system cloaked in darkness to keep you from knowing the truth. Even now, as you read this book, you know something is not right, and it hasn't been right for a long time. And the rich keep getting richer.

Silence. (Black Codes)

On April 26, 2022, President Joe Biden granted pardons to 3 people and shortened the sentences of 75 more nonviolent drug offenders trying to make the laws fair to all. But he has a long way to go.

https://www.npr.org/2022/04/26/1094755907/reentry-recidivism-biden-formerly-incarcerated-jobs-housing-healthcare-loans

In 1991, Biden Touts Work W/ Sen. Thurmond To Pass Strict Crack Cocaine Penalties

Joe Biden: If you have a piece of crack cocaine no bigger than this quarter that

I'm holding in my hand one quarter of one dollar we passed a law through leadership of Senator Thurman and myself and others a law that says if you get caught with that you go to jail for 5 years you get no probation you get nothing other than 5 years in jail, judge doesn't have a choice and under the forfeiture statures you can the government can take everything you own everything from your car to your house your bank account not merely what they confiscate in terms of the dollars from transaction you just got caught engaging in they can take everything

I don't care why *they* become a sociopath we have an obligation to corner them off from the rest of society *they* are in jail! Away from my mother your husband our families so I don't want to ask what made them do this they must be taken of the street!


https://www.youtube.com/watch?v=Ny lTKobMUiE

# TAKE A DEEP BREATH

# PART 2

# Melt Down

"Dead people …

and we have many examples

filled out ballots made applications
and then voted

which is even worse in other words …
dead people went through a process

some of them been dead for 25 years.
Millions of votes cast illegally
in swing states alone."

Witness Donald Trump a man that has lost his mind.

A desperate and stupid man, an embarrassment to the country.

A despot.

A friendless man who ran for President as a hoax and won.

A compulsive, unloved, and lonely man who learned nothing from his first impeachment who would be impeached a second time for inciting an insurrection.

The worse president in American history.

His only concern is for himself, TV ratings and staying in 'Power. This is a man who has lived 74 lying and unconscionable years... and, who at this moment knows he's totally fucked!

https://www.youtube.com/watch?v=WP0ixjE7JIU

President Donald Trump: (00:00)

Thank you. This may be the most important speech I've ever made.

I want to provide an update on our ongoing efforts to expose the tremendous voter fraud and irregularities which took place during the ridiculously long November 3rd elections.

We used to have what was called, election day.

Now we have election days, weeks, and months, and lots of bad things happened during this ridiculous period of time, especially when you have to prove almost nothing to exercise our greatest privilege, the right to vote.

As President, I have no higher duty than to defend the laws and the Constitution of the United States.

That is why I am determined to protect our election system, which is now under coordinated assault and siege.

President Donald Trump: (00:54)

For months, leading up to the Presidential election, we were warned that we should not declare a premature victory. We were told repeatedly that it would take weeks if not, months, to determine the winner, to count the absentee ballots and to verify the results.

My opponent was told to stay away from the election, don't campaign.

"We don't need you. We've got it.

This election is done." In fact, they were acting like they already knew what the outcome was going to be.

They had it covered and perhaps they did, very sadly for our country.

It was all very, very strange. Within days after the election, we witnessed an orchestrated effort to anoint the winner even while many key states were still being counted.


Full transcript (at end of book)

# Total Nut Case

"There were many moments

that were comedy,

though tragic comedy…"


Michael Luttig




Sara Cooper Impersonates Donald
Trump


"No that's her with the gold.

I better use some Tick Tacks in case

I start kissing her I'm auto attracted to beautiful I just start kissing them it's like a magnet

I just kiss I don't even wait when you a star they let you do it."

https://twitter.com/MisterSalesman/status/1321991030242185219

Donald Trump: And I tested …

very positively in a another sense so…

this morning yeah I tested positively toward

negative right so no uh …

I tested perfectly this morning …
meaning


meaning I tested negative.


https://twitter.com/MisterSalesman/status/1333248450285215746


I knew the truth would come out sooner
or later


about Trump's campaign lawyer.


This woman says she's Jenna Ellis law
mentor.

"I have different philosophy when it comes to the

law like when it comes to the evidence some

people say show your evidence

 I say don't show your evidence that's for you,

You don't have to show nobody the evidence."

https://twitter.com/sarahcpr/status/1332491832786350080

I said is there a cognitive test and he said there actually is and he named it whatever it might be it was 30 or 35

the first questions are very easy the last
questions are much more difficult like a
memory question it's a you person
woman man camera TV


okay so they say can you repeat that


So I say yea person woman man camera
TV okay that's very good if you get in
order you get extra points okay now he's
asking you other questions then 10 min
or 15 minutes or 20 min later they say
you remember that first question not the
first the 10<sup>th</sup> question give us that again
can you do that again person woman
man camera TV if you get it in order you
get extra points

I said person woman man camera TV if you get in order you get extra points he said nobody gets it's not the easy but for me it was easy and that's not an easy question in other words if you repeat them and it's out of order it's okay but not as good that but then when you go back 20 to 25 minutes later and they say go back to question and repeat them can you do it?

Person woman man camera TV and they say that's amazing how did you do that?

I do it because I have a good memory and because I am cognitively there.

https://twitter.com/sarahcpr/status/1286675192585093126

https://twitter.com/MisterSalesman/sta
tus/1332518287247355905

# How Fascism Will Come

*"When fascism comes, it will greet us with a smile." -T Ehret*

In the darkness of the night, a figure approaches,

A force so dark and sinister it sends chills down our spine.

Fascism is its name, and it seeks to consume,

To sit for tea with the governor of Florida in a cozy room. I want to be president.

From California to Tennessee, it defiles
mosques with disdain,


Chanting its message, "Wake up,
America, the enemy is here."


It will sing praises of God. I'm a
Christian Nationalist and hold rallies
across the country


Vilify and monopolize, with no
realization.


Interviewed on podcasts, it smiles with
glee,


Lovingly embraced by those who can't
see,

Its talking points rehearsed, its Tweets
well crafted,

A disdain for big words and too many
syllables, it laughs as its drafted.

Books are shredded, knowledge burned,

Its message is clear, there is nothing to
be learned.

Teachers are condemned, unions
outlawed,

No dissent shall be heard, no voice
allowed.

The darkness of fascism creeps in, inch
by inch,

A force so powerful, it's hard to pinch.

But let us not forget the lessons of
history,


To stand against tyranny, to fight for our
liberty.


We must unite against this foe,


To preserve our democracy, to let our
voices flow.


Let us embrace knowledge, education,
and truth,


And say no to fascism with our voices
uncouth.

For fascism shall not prevail,

Its darkness shall not our freedom assail.

We stand united against its power,


To fight for what is right every hour.


So let us stand up and say no to fascism,


To its pissing-ass tea parties, its
destruction, and its schism.


We are the guardians of democracy, and
we shall not fail,


Our voices shall be heard, and our
resistance shall prevail.

# This Was Not a Movie

*"All tyrannies rule through 'Fraud and Force, once the fraud is exposed, they must rely on Force."*

**George Orwell*

We are going to recommend you for criminal prosecution ... "You, Sir, are a liar, a manipulator, a cheat, and a traitor."

But I'm not a Crook! And I'm not a Drunk!!!!"  X

The Mueller Report, the Ukraine Bribe, Georgia phone call to overturn the election, the January 6 insurrection, and

the stealing of Classified Documents —
something far more sinister is going on.

Liz Cheney: Do you believe the violence
on Jan 6 was justified morally?

Flynn:  I take the Fifth.

Cheney: Do you believe the violence on
Jan 6 was justified legally?

Flynn: I plead the Fifth.

Cheney: Do you believe in the peaceful
transition of power in the United States
of America?

Flynn:  The Fifth.

Mitch McConnell, "I'm not an impartial juror." "This is a political process. There is not anything judicial about it. Impeachment is a political ... "We will have a largely partisan outcome. There is no chance Donald Trump will be removed." The first Impeachment trial obstruction of Congress and abuse of power. Twice Impeached.

Mueller Report

Trump: There is no collusion. He said no conclusion.

George:  He didn't say there was no collusion.


Trump:  He said no collusion, George the report said <u>no collusion</u>." Let me underline that <u>no collusion)</u>…


George: Did you read the report?


Trump: uh …Yes I did.


Robert Mueller confirms crimes in the report


*Trump:  It's a whole big fat hoax it's just a hoax.*


Robert Mueller: No it's not hoax.

*Trump: It's a total witch hunt.*

Mueller:  It is not a witch-hunt.

*Trump: There was no obstruction and if you
read the report, you'll see that.*

Nadler:  The report did conclude that he
did not commit obstruction of justice. Is
that correct?

Mueller:  That is correct.

*Trump: It was a complete and total exoneration.*

Nadler:  Did you actually totally
exonerate the president?

Mueller:  No.

Rep. Ken Buck: Could you charge the
president with a crime after he left
office?

Mueller:  Yes.

Buck:  You believe he committed … you
could charge the president of the United
States of America with obstruction
justice after he left office?

Mueller:  Yes. Our investigation of
efforts to obstruct the investigation and
lied to investigators were of critical
importance.

Donald Trump's "dog whistle" started way back, at the start of the pandemic, when he tweeted in code to militant groups (Storm the state capitols)

LIBERATE VIRGINIA, and save your great 2nd Amendment. It is under siege!

LIBERATE MICHIGAN!

LIBERATE MINNESOTA!

# They All Knew

"They all knew then

and they all know now."

Lindsey Graham:  I want to talk to the Trump supporters for a minute I don't know who you are or why you like this guy.  He's a race baiting xenophobic religious bigot.  I think he's a kook. I think he's crazy. I think he is unfit for office.

Ted Cruz: Whatever he does he accuses everyone else of doing. The man cannot tell the truth but he combines it with being a narcissist racist, a narcissist at a level I don't this country have ever seen. He doesn't know the difference between truth and lies. He lies practically every word that comes out of his mouth.

Rand Paul: And my concern is that he would grab up that power and really treat the country as sort of his little bully fiefdom. Donald Trump is a delusional narcissist and an orange faced windbag.

Nikki Haley: Donald Trump is everything I taught my children not to do in kindergarten.

Marco Rubio: He's been exploiting working Americans for forty years. Donald Trump is a con artist.

Kellyanne Conway: He says he's for the little guy but he's actually built a lot of

his businesses on the backs of the little
guy.

Mike Pompeo: You know, Donald
Trump the other day said "if he tells a
solider to commit a war crime the solider
would just go do it."

Glenn Beck: And I don't think Donald
Trump has even read the constitution
knows what's in the constitution.

Rick Perry: A toxic mix of demagoguery
and mean spiritedness and nonsense.

Susan Collins: I just cannot support
Donald Trump.

https://twitter.com/MisterSalesman/status/1539107800034451457

# Pressure Point

"When exposing a crime is treated as committing

a crime, you are being ruled by criminals."

--Edward Snowden

"Just say that the election was corrupt + leave the rest to me and the R. Congressmen," Trump said on the call, according to acting Attorney General Donoghue's notes.

Rudy Giuliani on Jan 6. "Who hides evidence.

Criminals hide evidence, not honest people.

So, over the next 10 days we get to see the

machines that are crooked, the ballots that are fraudulent, and if we're wrong, we will be made fools of.  But if we're right a lot of them will go to jail. So, let's have trial by combat.

https://www.youtube.com/watch?v=mh3cbd7niTQ

Former Trump adviser Peter Navarro on being charged for contempt of Congress for defying a January 6th Committee subpoena.

Peter Navarro, "They intercepted me gettin' on the plane and then they put me in handcuffs, they bring me here. They put me in leg irons. They stick me in a cell."

https://twitter.com/therecount/status/1532824728494387200

Republican Minority leader Kevin McCarthy, Mo Brooks, Jim Jordan, and Scott Perry also refuses to comply with subpoenas.

Four days after the insurrection reports surfaced that Kevin McCarthy GOP Minority Leader wanted Donald Trump to resign.

Kevin called the report totally false and wrong and that he never wanted Trump to resign.

And then The New York Times dropped the bomb. They released McCarthy's recordings in his voice.

*Kevin McCarthy GOP leader in a private call to a Republican Senators.*

*"But let me be very clear to all of you and I have been very clear to the President. He bears responsibility for his words and actions.*

*No if, ands or buts.  I asked him personally today, does he hold responsibility for what happened? Does he feel bad to what happened? He told me that he does have some responsibility for what happened. And he needs to acknowledge that. I've had it with this guy. What he did was is unacceptable.*


https://www.youtube.com/watch?v=P87Y-K9Tlv4


*What I think I'm going to do is, I'm going to call him. This, this is what I think. We know it'll pass the House. I think there is a chance it'll pass the house Senate, even when he's gone. Um, and I think there is a lot of different ramifications for that. Now I haven't a discussion with the Dems that if he did resign, would that happen? Now, this is one personal fear that I have. I don't want to get into any conversation about Pence pardoning him. Again, the only discussions I was going to have with him is that I think this will pass, and it would be my recommendation you should resign.*

https://www.youtube.com/watch?v=P8
7Y-K9Tlv4

# FAILED COUP

"Your lies won't protect you."


"I never gave a tour of the Capitol on
Jan 5, 2021."


Barry Loudermilk was one of the 139
representatives and 8 senators who voted
to overturn democracy on January 6.


 On the day before the insurrection,
Surveillance footage shows a tour led by
Republican Loudermilk to areas in the
House Office Buildings and the
entrances to Capitol tunnels.

Individuals on the tour photographed/recorded areas not typically of interest to tourists: hallways, staircases and security checkpoints.

https://twitter.com/January6thCmte/status/1537075019918065666

Republican Congressman Loudermilk is shown giving a surveillance tour a day before the insurrection. Why were they taking photos of stairwells and doors?

https://twitter.com/January6thCmte/status/1537075019918065666

147 Republicans voted against democracy on January 6, 2021.

Steve Bannon walks into courthouse, a man walks behind him with a 'Failed Coup' sign.

Judge rejects Steve Bannon's motion to dismiss the indictment for defying J6 Committee's subpoena. He has no defense, he'll go to trial, get convicted and go to prison.

# The Worst of the Worst

*"We are living through what feels like the end of America" Ginni Thomas*

Ginni Thomas, the wife of Supreme Court Justice Clarence Thomas, sent 21 text messages to Trump's Chief of Staff, Mark Meadows, to encourage him to overthrow the election. One of Meadows replies:

"This is a fight of good versus evil," Meadows texted Ginni Thomas, "Evil always looks like the victor until the King of Kings triumphs. Do not grow weary in well doing. The fight continues. I have staked my career on it."

Jefferey Clark, a DOJ official said that he would send letters to the state legislators to change the electoral votes if Trump appointed him Attorney General.

"History is calling," Clark told the president, according to a deposition from Donoghue in a court filing. "This is our opportunity. We can get this done."

Clark's bosses had warned there was no election fraud. Trump told his DOJ officials that he didn't care just say there was and leave the rest to me and my Republican friends in Congress.

"And seeing that Jefferey Clark was going along with Trump's treasonous plot, Richard Donoghue told Clark there is no election fraud … "That's right.

You're an environment lawyer. What if you go back to your office and we'll call you if there is an oil spill…"


A year later, Jeffery Clark pleaded the 5th before the J6 Committee.


https://dianeravitch.net/2022/06/19/the-most-shocking-story-yet-about-the-failed-coup/


•


The January 6th Committee has obtained post-election emails between JOHN EASTMAN & GINNI THOMAS, the wife of Supreme Court Justice, Clarence Thomas.  The two referenced overturning the 2020 election.  Justice Clarence Thomas tried to block those emails from being turned over to the committee.

https://www.youtube.com/watch?app=desktop&v=txN_Cf7NYDo

Hakeem Jeffries is fucking done with Clarence & Ginni Thomas.  Listen to what he had to say.

https://twitter.com/RepJeffries/status/1524444222497169411

# May God Be with Us

*"These tragedies have reminded us that words*

*matter and that the power of life*

*and death is in the tongue."*

Oh, I can scarce believe my ears,
And what is being said, I fear.

Our country's torn, so weak and worn,
Worshipping a man, so greatly adorned.

It's like a drug, a toxic glee,

73 million lost, can't you see?

But this is not the first we've been,

A microcosm of history, repeating again.


Folks don't know the half of it,

If only we could see a bit,


Back in time, to understand,

And make the changes, take a stand.


Oh, how I'd give it all away,


For just one ride, one chance to say,

"I'll save the world, I'll make it right,"


With eyes on the past, to end this fright.

And you got those Congressmen turning
the House of Representatives into the
House of Evilness


In the halls of power, where laws are
made,

The House of Representatives, once
esteemed, now degraded.


For some Congressmen have turned
from the light,


Their actions now stained, filling it with
evil's might.


Once a place of dignity, where
democracy was wrought,

Now twisted by greed, its purpose has been sought.

The halls that echoed with the voice of the people's choice,

Now resonate with lies, concealing corruption's voice.

Oh how the mighty have fallen, what a sight to see,

The House of Representatives, now the House of Evilness, oh so sadly.

No longer a bastion of truth, no longer a beacon of hope,

It's a place where integrity is lost, and lies
and deceit they cope.


Kevin McCarthy, Marjorie Taylor Green,
Matt Gates, George Santos, Jim Jordan,
Lindsey Graham, Ted Cruz, Lauren
Boebert


So let us remember this dark chapter in
our land,


And strive to reclaim the House, with
truth and honor in hand.


For the future of democracy, depends on
this great hall,


And we must ensure it remains, standing
tall, once and for all.

# January 6, 2021

Isaiah 46:9  "They lavish gold out of the bag, and weigh silver in the balance, and hire a goldsmith; and he maketh it a god: they fall down, yea, they worship. Remember this, and shew yourselves men.. bring it again to mind, O ye transgressors."

The angry mob chanted,

'Hang Mike Pence,' 'Hang Mike Pence.'

"Thanks to your bullshit, we are under siege,"

Jacob wrote to John Eastman during the insurrection.


*Seven people died that day on January 6, including two police officers, and two would die days later from suicide.*


Now, look at the criminal trial of Charles Manson in 1969. Prosecutors acknowledged Manson was neither present at the murders nor had he explicitly ordered them. According to the case put forward at trial, Manson did not need to explicitly command anything in order for cult members to know what it was that he wanted them to do.


Charles Manson was convicted on 7 counts of murder & 1 count of conspiracy to commit murder.

And then there was The BK Killer, August 18, 2005, who murdered ten people. He was sentenced to life in prison without the possibility of parole for 175 years.

So why is the Jan 6 Killer allowed to roam free?

Trump: All Pence has to do is send it back to the states to recertify and we become President & you are the happiest people.  "These were peaceful people the love the love in the air I never saw anything like it."

A rioter said, "I'm not allowed to say what's going to happen today because everyone just has to watch, but it's going to happen; something is going to happen one way or the other."

Something did happen, and it was supposed to be a lot worse.

https://twitter.com/Bill_Maxwell_/status/1535292597983334400



https://www.youtube.com/watch?v=mWzYB2RmfPU

# The Monsters Come Out of Hiding

Roger Stone, "This is nothing but an
epic struggle


for the future of the country between
dark and


light, between the godly and the godless
between


good and evil.  We will win this fight or
America


will step off into a thousand years of
darkness."

https://www.c-span.org/video/?c5023345/user-clip-tangled-web-deceit

Trump on Roger Stone before the pardon.

https://www.youtube.com/watch?v=FHUJ29AjaHI

Republican Senators were in on the coup plotting.

Ali Alexander posted a video before the Jan 6 attack.

"I'm the person who came up with the Jan 6 idea with Republican Congressmen Paul Gosar, Mo Brooks, Andy Biggs.

We four schemed up of putting maximum pressure on Congress while they were voting so we could change their minds and they could hear our loud roar from outside."

https://twitter.com/grantstern/status/1546938420223672320

Steve Bannon awaiting trial for defying a subpoena from Congress:

"Pray for our enemies, because we're going medieval on these people. We're gonna savage our enemies…."

https://twitter.com/jason_paladino/status/1347647000922230784

# Public Hearings

# Day: 1

*"Nobody died during Watergate, nor was anyone beaten." John Dean*

IVANKA: "I accepted what AG Barr was saying (that election theft claims were 'BULLSHIT')"

Trump said, "Mike Pence, 'Deserves' to Be Hanged.

Liz Chaney and Scott Perry and other Republican Senators asked the Donald Trump for pardons in the days after the Jan 6 insurrection.

Liz Cheney in her opening statement…
"Not only did President Trump refuse to tell the mob to  leave the Capitol he placed no call to any elements of the US Government to instruct that the Capitol to be defended.

- He did not call his Defense Secretary on January 6, he did not talk to his Attorney General, he did not talk to Homeland Security. He did not give an order to deploy the National Guards that day.

- He made no effort to work with Department of Justice that day and to deploy law enforcement assets… but the Vice President, Mike Pence did each of those things."

Trump on Jan 6: "I hope Mike does the right thing… I hope so I hope so "Because if Mike Pence does the right thing, we win the election.  All Vice President has to do is it back to states to recertify and we become President you will be the happiest people and if he doesn't that will be a sad day for country. Mike Pence I hope you're going to stand up for the good of our Constitution and for the good of our country and if you're not I'm going to be very disappointed in you and I will tell you right now."

https://www.youtube.com/watch?v=6VncJkZxnRk&list=PLDIVi-vBsOEyKUzsOa4jacKVDQsk3U1b1&index=4

https://www.cnn.com/videos/politics/2022/06/09/new-produced-video-capitol-riot-2022-january-6-hearings-vpx.cnn/video/playlists/the-january-6-hearings/

# Day: 2

"I told him it was bullshit." Bill Barr

"Right out of the box on election night, the President claimed that there was major fraud underway. I mean, this happened, as far as I could tell, before there was actually any potential of looking at evidence." -- Attorney General Bill Barr

"I told him that the stuff his people were shoveling out to the public was bullshit." -- Bill Barr

"Not the approach I would take if I were you." -- Jared Kushner

"Mr. Trump decided before the election...that he would claim it was rigged." -- Zoe Lofgren


"I don't know that I had a firm view of what he should say." -- Ivanka Trump


According to testimonies, Rudy Giuliani was drunk on election night and told Trump to declare victory.  'We won. They're stealing it from us ... we need to go say that we won.'


The Big Lie was Born:  Knowingly and willfully.

Trump's speech on Election Night 2020.

"This is a fraud on the American public.

This is an embarrassment to our country

We were getting ready to win this election… frankly, we did win this election.

So, our goal now is to ensure the integrity for the good of this nation..."

We want all voting to stop we don't want

them to add any ballots at 4:00 in the morning

and add them to the list okay?

It's a very sad moment to me it's a very
sad

moment … and we will win this and as
far as

I'm concern we already have won it."

<u>https://youtu.be/YlmaKdbC6ZM?t=36
1</u>

Trump sent out as many as 25
fundraising emails a day, for an 'Election
Defense Fund' that didn't exist, to small
dollar donors. They raised $250 million
dollars in just a few weeks.

# Day: 3

The Devil We Know ... put so much heat on Mike Pence that he was lucky he didn't burn up. So why isn't he testifying? He can't hurt you now.  Nail him Mike don't let him get away.

https://twitter.com/MisterSalesman/status/1537984834508730370

Ginni Thomas, wife of Supreme Court Justice Clarence Thomas sends emails to John Eastman about overturning the election.

John Eastman: Says he has inside knowledge about secret, heated discussions between SCOTUS justices.

Eric Hershman, White House lawyer, on John

Eastman call after January 6 plot to overturn the election results. "I told him are you out of your fucking mind? I only want to hear two words coming out of your mouth from now on. Orderly transition. Repeat those words…

Orderly transition.  Good John.

Now I'm going to give you the best free legal advice you are ever getting in your life... get a  great f''cking criminal defense lawyer, you're going to need it.

John Eastman, who advised Donald Trump on overturning the 2020 election, sought a pardon from Rudy Giuliani after the Capitol riot, the Jan. 6 panel said.

"I've decided that I should be on the pardon list, if that is still in the works," Eastman wrote to Giuliani in an email sent on Jan. 11, 2021, that was shown during Thursday's testimony. "Will taint me, but given the outright lies and false witness being spewed, having that protection is probably the prudent."

A year later, John Eastman testified to the committee and pled the 5th over 100 times. So, did he get a pocket pardon from Trump? And what about Rudy Giuliani, Donald Jr., Ivanka & her husband Jared, they testified and didn't plead the 5th.

# Day: 4

"Our world is not divided by race, color, gender or religion. Our world is divided into wise people and fools. And fools divide themselves by race, color, gender, or religion." --Mohamad Safa

I was in tears. What Trump did to Ruby Freeman and her daughter is evil personified! "The only protection the FBI gave her was to run for 2 months. Yet Congress gave Supreme Court Justices around the clock security from pro-choice protesters outside their homes.

Trump's Big Lie ruined people's lives.

"I lost my name I lost my reputation I've lost my sense of security all because a group of people starting with a group of people starting with #45 and his ally Rudy Giuliani decided to scapegoat me and my daughter Shaye to push their own lies how the presidential election was stolen. There is nowhere that I feel save. Nowhere. Do you know how it feels to have the President of the United States to target you? The President o the United States is suppose represent every American, not to target one, but he targeted me Lady Ruby a small business owner, a mother a proud America citizen who stands up to help run an election in Fulton county in the middle of a pandemic."

https://www.youtube.com/watch?v=xw2yxupsLT0

Nasty lies spread by Donald Trump and his allies destroyed their lives.

Shae Moss full testimony

https://www.youtube.com/watch?v=-EKbwg1fQ3w

Trump issued a statement minutes before Arizona House Speaker, Rusty Bowers testimony and called him a RINO...

https://youtu.be/hPhpcSuGEX8?t=47

# Day: 5

Liz Cheney in Day:1 said Congressman Scott Perry contacted the White House after Jan 6 to seek a pardon. He called it "a ludicrous and soulless lie.'

Day 5: The Committee showed the evidence...

https://www.youtube.com/watch?v=WdnUNKw2cZ0&list=PLDIVi-vBsOEyETRGoRP9y8zhyu6bHl6iK&index=3

"More than a dozen DOJ law enforcement officials searched Jeffery Clark's house in a pre-dawn raid, put him in the streets in his PJs, for 3 1/2 hours, and took his electronic devices." The noose is tightening around Trump's conspirators.

"Are we a Monarchy or a Republic?" "A Republic if you can keep it." Only a king can pardon someone from cradle to grave for all manner of crimes. And only a King can pardon himself. "Long live the King."

Eric Herschmann: Rep Matt Gaetz asked for a pardon "The pardon he was requesting was as broad as you could describe, from the beginning of time, up until today, for any and all things."

Just call the election corrupt and leave the rest to me and my R Congressmen

https://www.youtube.com/watch?v=DJtRtWu7gcE

# Day: 6

*"Trump grabbed the steering wheel and lunged at a Secret Service agent trying to get to the Capitol on January 6."*

The Star Witness, Cassidy Hutchinson

"I noticed the head of Mr. Trump's security detail sitting in a chair, looking somewhat discombobulated, a little lost,"

Hutchinson testified. "I looked at Tony, he said, 'Did you effing hear what happened in the Beast?'

I said, 'No, Tony, I just got back, what happened?'

"As the president had gotten into the vehicle with Bobby, he thought that they were going up to the Capitol. And when Bobby had relayed to him that we're not; we don't have the assets to do it; it's not secure; we're going back to the West Wing, the president had a very strong, very angry response to that."

Hutchinson then testified that Trump said, 'I'm the effing president, take me up to the Capitol now,'" to which Bobby responded, "Sir, we have to go back to the West Wing."

https://twitter.com/Reuters/status/15418597216065822277

https://www.youtube.com/watch?v=89yd3q_geMk

Donald Trump posted 12 times on his platform. He called Cassidy Hutchinson every name under the sun, a familiar pattern… "I don't know this woman not my type bad news total phony vote scammer hustler third rate social climber fake liar loser thug."

Cassidy Hutchinson is under OATH, on Capitol Hill ... and you, Sir, are on Truth Social where the truth goes to die.  You "are the phony, the fake, and bad news." Even Fox News knows it.

https://twitter.com/RonFilipkowski/status/1541899130813005833

Cassidy said to Mark Meadows, "I just had a conversation with Rudy, sounds like we're going to the Capitol?

Meadows said, "There's a lot going on Cass, but I don't know things might get real real bad on Jan 6."

House Rep Majority Leader Kevin McCarthy called Cassidy Hutchinson on January 6, "Don't come up here... The president just said he's marching to the Capitol. You told me this whole week you aren't coming up here, why would you lie to me?"

Cassidy testified, "I didn't lie to you."

When Trump was told about the crowd had weapons: "I don't f-ing care that they have weapons. They're not here to hurt me. Take the f-ing metal detectors away. Let my people in. They can march

to the Capitol from here. Let them in
Take the f-ing mags away."


White House lawyer, Pat Cipollone to
Mark Meadows. "Mark, we need to do
something more... They're literally
calling for the vice president to be f-ing
hung!"


"And Mark had responded something to
the effect of, 'You heard him, Pat, he
thinks Mike deserves it. (Trump) He
doesn't think they're doing anything
wrong." (Hang Mike Pence) (Hang Mike
Pence)"


Pat Cipollone said, "Please make sure we
don't go to the Capitol, Cassidy. Keep in
touch with me we're going to get charged

with every f""king crime imaginable if we make that move happen."

"Mark, something needs to be done or people are going to die & the blood is going to be on your f---ing hands. This is getting out of control I'm going down there."

Meadows said, "He doesn't want to do anything."

# Day: 7

Jan. 6 Committee links Trump allies Roger Stone and Michael Flynn to White Supremacists' Militant Groups through chat group 'Friends of Stone.'

https://www.youtube.com/watch?v=iA2O2DpC16w

Liz Cheney said Donald Trump knew exactly what he was doing. "He is a 76-year-old man and not an impressionable child. Just like everyone else in our country, he is responsible for his own actions and his own choices."

Cheney added: "Donald Trump cannot escape responsibility by being willfully blind."

"Trump had access to more detailed and specific information showing that the election was not actually stolen than almost any other American."

https://www.youtube.com/watch?v=T5D5mavXdiI

Capitol rioter Stephen Ayres said that Trump's words incited the supporters and who then attacked the Capitol on Jan. 6.

"We basically were just following what he said. – and it ruined my life, had I known that Donald Trump knew that the election was not stolen I never would have come to Washington, DC.”

Jason Van Tatenhove, former Oath Keeper Spokesman said,

“We were lucky that day. They had gallows set up for Vice President Mike Pence. What else is Donald Trump going to do if he gets elected again? That's a scary notion. I have 3 daughters and a granddaughter, and I fear for the world that they will inherit if we don't start holding these people to account.”

https://twitter.com/washingtonpost/status/1546960430563835905

Trump: 'I don't want to say the Election is over.'

https://www.youtube.com/watch?v=0j9XgBAeRIs&list=PLzWYN9o77i8dwTQ57UeOBVZ6oPKfSAL-m&index=7

Trump's edits to the Jan 7th draft speech that he didn't want to say.

.

https://www.youtube.com/watch?v=qNiQoUqvsR0

<u>Depositions</u>

Jan 6 Investigator: Do know what this is?

Ivanka Trump: It looks like draft remarks for that day."

Investigator: There are words crossed out & some words added.

Do you recognize the handwriting?

Ivanka: "It looks like my father's handwriting."

Investigator: It looks here like he crossed out 'that all lawbreakers will be prosecuted to the fullest extent of the law. We must send a clear message not with mercy but with justice. Legal consequences must be swift and firm.'

Do you know why he wanted that crossed out?

Jared Kushner:  I don't know.

Investigator:  He also crossed out. 'I want to be clear; you do not represent me. You do not represent our movement.'

Do you know why he crossed that language out of the statement?

Jared:  I don't know.

https://twitter.com/RepElaineLuria/status/1551568001836670976


"For three hours, seven minutes." While the attack was happening and people were dying, Donald Trump watched it unfold on Fox News.


Do you know where the President was while the attack on the Capitol was going on?


"In the dining room watching television."

<u>https://twitter.com/RepKinzinger/statu</u>
<u>s/1550107400232992768</u>

Donald Trump's last tweet, on Jan 6.

"Remember this day forever!"

Adam Kinzinger said, "He showed absolutely no remorse for the officers injured and died that day."

# Witness Intimidation is a Crime

Liz Cheney: After our last hearing, President Trump tried to call a witness in our investigation, a witness you have yet not seen in these hearings,

"That person declined to answer or respond to President Trump's call, and instead alerted their lawyer... and their lawyer alerted us. This committee has supplied that information to the Dept. of Justice."

https://twitter.com/ABC/status/15469 47967466307585

At the end of Day 6 Public Hearing, Liz Cheney revealed text messages of witness intimidation by Mark Meadows associates.

"(A person) let me know you have your deposition tomorrow. He wants me to let you know that he's thinking about you. He knows you're loyal and you're going to do the right thing when you go in for your deposition.

"What they said to me is as long as I continue to be a team player, they know that I'm on the team, I'm doing the right thing, I'm protecting who I need to protect, you know, I'll continue to stay in good graces in Trump World.

And they have reminded me a couple of times that Trump does read transcripts and just to keep that in mind as I proceed through my depositions and interviews with the committee."

https://www.youtube.com/watch?v=z5HT8SFiB_8

Bennie Thompson concluded, "Because of this courageous woman and others like her, your attempt to hide the truth from the American people will fail."

https://twitter.com/ifindkarma/status/1542027943311839232

# The Battle at Kruger

*"We may ignore, but we can nowhere evade, the presence of*

*God. The world is crowded with him. He walks everywhere*

*incognito." -C.S. Lewis*

Our Democracy hangs in the balance like never before, but don't think that evil will win for one moment.

*youtu.be/LU8DDYz68kM*

# Clear and Present Danger

"Donald Tump, his allies, and supporters

are a clear and present danger to
American Democracy. " Michael Luttig


In the 1961 movie, Pressure Point,
starring Sidney Poitier as a medical
doctor, he interviewed a psychopath who
was charged   with seditious conspiracy
to overthrow the government.


"What drives you to say things like that
that?"


"Politics."

"So, you really expect to win like that?
Look where it has gotten you so far in

jail. You expect to use violence to overthrow the government? "

"Well, that's up to the American people, depends on the people what they are willing to do."

https://www.youtube.com/watch?v=EC6bZLV5bOI&t=594s

On January 15, 2022, Judge Luttig testified at public hearing that Trump, his allies' and supporters continue to spread lies and misinformation and represent "a clear and present danger to democracy."

https://www.youtube.com/watch?v=tpKI12L1bEI

Two days later, on June 17, 2022, Trump gave a speech at the Faith and Freedom Coalition and lambasted and derided Mike Pence for not helping him overthrow the government and made a mockery of the constitution.


Clear and Present Danger to our democracy


https://twitter.com/atrupar/status/1537894001746948097


Senator Lindsey Graham spoke about what he like about Donald Trump— being a bully. He liked that.

https://twitter.com/therecount/status/1537836681486905345

# The Lawless Citizen

On August 8, 2022, the FBI searched Donald Trump's residence in an 'F'ck around with us and see what happens in an unprecedented move.

Trump announced, "My beautiful home, Mar-A-Lago in Palm Beach, Florida, is currently under siege, raided and occupied by a large group of FBI agents."

"They even broke into my safe."

Immediately afterward, Trump emailed his supporters, grifting them for money.

MSNBC host Lawrence O'Donnell said he  got a fundraiser email from Donald J Trump that said 'Mar-a-Lago was raided. Please rush in a donation immediately.' He even suggests a donation. "He thinks I'm good for $45.00."

https://www.youtube.com/watch?v=7O tvdntUKtM

Watch the parallels between Trump and the character Satan — in the 1997 movie the Devil's Advocate. They shot the character's home at Trump Tower in Trump's residence.

"Vanity is my favorite sin."

On August 9, 2022, one day after the FBI searched his home, Trump pleaded the Fifth 440 times in New York Attorney General's investigation into Trump Organization's business dealings.

Trump once said, "The mob takes the Fifth.  If you're innocent, why are you taking the Fifth Amendment? I think it's disgraceful. Horrible. Horrible."

Rudy Giuliani is in the sh't house. ' Judge suggests Rudy Giuliani travel by train or 'Uber or whatever' after his lawyers said a medical issue prevents him from flying to Atlanta to testify in a Trump election probe.'

Trump: "Rudy Giuliani is great. He's got guts, unlike many in the Republican Party. The Eliot Ness of his generation and one of the "greatest crime fighters" the US has ever known."

—Donald Trump's last good words about Rudy a year earlier.

What happened to Rudy?  Ken Frydman told Ari on MSNBC that Donald Trump stole Rudy Giuliani's soul… "Rudy let him. He got seduced by the money, power, access, and fame. His goal for him and Trump-- disrupt the world and create chaos."

https://www.youtube.com/watch?app=desktop&v=EVoHXoGa0nU

Fulton County, GA Judge Robert McBurney rejects Rudy Giuliani's claim that he cannot fly to appear in court due to health concerns:

"John Madden drove all over the country ... One thing we need to explore is whether Mr. Giuliani can get here ... on a train, or on a bus, or Uber."  "I'm confident he can figure out a way — short of a Greyhound — to get him to Atlanta. X  "Do it in 3 legs. [Do] you know folks in DC? Spend the night there."

https://twitter.com/therecount/status/1557086466517438464

Senator Lindsey Graham is also on his way to testify in Georgia Probe after the Judge denied his request to "Quash" the subpoena.

Michael Cohen said, "There is going to be so much flipping, it's going to be like watching a Gymnastic event."  Watch the video.

https://www.youtube.com/watch?v=xm8Fy-g1f6g

https://www.youtube.com/watch?v=sRJLJFLQVYk

It's one thing to say you don't like Flipping but it's another thing to say cooperating with the FBI should be illegal for telling what you know about someone.

Watch the interview with Donald Trump.

*https://www.youtube.com/watch?v=cLBZb2tw8V0*

# Who Snitched on Donald?

Who was the mold at Mar-A-Lago that snitched on Donald Trump? Who told the FBI what and where to find the Top Secret documents he stole from the White House?

Sources say some documents were classified information about nuclear weapons.  Was it Trump's children, his son-in law, or his wife?

Watch the video by the Lincoln Project.

https://www.youtube.com/watch?v=Gc VSC-

BgTww&list=RDCMUCpYCxV51bykh
MY-wSUozQRg&start_radio=1

'Insiders say it was Kushner and Melanie
pointed to as possible Moles in FBI raid'

https://www.independent.co.uk/news/
world/americas/us-politics/donald-
trump-fbi-raid-melania-
b2143194.html?utm_term=Autofeed&ut
m_campaign=IndyUS&utm_medium=S
ocial&utm_source=Twitter#Echobox=1
660248636


THE FBI FOUND TSSCI
DOCUMENTS  TOP SECRET
SENSITIVE COMPARTMENTED
INFORMATION

https://www.youtube.com/watch?v=zo
v-IdKVKUs

# Trump's Motive

So why did Donald Trump go to great lengths to steal top secret government documents, lie, cover up, and obstruct justice, knowing the consequences can be severe?

One possible explanation is to look at the minds of serial killers.

Serial killers are narcissists and psychopaths who often keep "souvenirs" of their victims. For example, the BTK Killer kept his victims' driver's licenses, and Ted Bundy took photographs, clothes, and jewelry. When asked about this behavior, Bundy explained, "When you work hard to do something right, you don't want to forget it.

This mindset of wanting to keep something as a trophy could be applied to people who steal government documents or lie to protect themselves. They may feel a sense of pride or accomplishment in obtaining sensitive information or covering up their tracks. They may also want to use this information as leverage or blackmail against others.

One high-profile example of this behavior is former President Donald Trump. Despite being advised by White House lawyers and advisors not to take boxes of documents to his Mar-a-Lago property, he reportedly said, "It's not theirs, it's mine." This statement suggests a possessive and entitled attitude towards information, similar to how serial killers view their "souvenirs" as personal belongings.

Of course, not everyone who engages in this type of behavior is a psychopath or serial killer. Other factors could be at play, such as a desire for power, control, or financial gain. However, the similarity in mindset between these individuals is worth examining.

Serial killers, when caught, face life in prison or even the death penalty. Meanwhile, individuals who steal government documents or obstruct justice may be imprisoned. The risks may not be enough to deter them, however, as their desire for information or control outweighs the potential consequences.

In conclusion, the minds of serial killers can offer some insight into why some individuals are willing to go to great lengths to obtain information or cover up their actions.

The desire for a "souvenir" or personal possession of sensitive information can motivate them, even if it means breaking the law. While not everyone who engages in this behavior is a narcissist or psychopath, or both, the mindset is worth examining and understanding to prevent future instances of theft or obstruction of justice. Although the consequences of these actions can be severe, the risks are not worth the reward.

After being charged with 34 felony counts in a New York court, former

President Donald Trump criticized multiple investigations he's facing and berated special counsel Jack Smith, who is investigating the stolen document case, was using a fake name. Trump even called him a lunatic. "This lunatic special prosecutor named Jack Smith - I wonder what it was prior to the change," Trump said as some folks in the audience laughed. But as they will see, this is not a joking matter.

# Merrick Garland

Donald Trump thought Merrick Garland rode in town on a donkey but discovered he was a "Dragon Slayer." David vs. Goliath Rule #1 "Never underestimate your opponent."

Good afternoon, since I became the Attorney General, I made it clear that the justice department will through its court filings and work.

Just now the Justice Department has filed a motion in the southern district of Florida to unseal a search warrant and property receipt relating to a court approved search that the FBI conducted earlier this week.

That search was on a premises located in Florida belonging to the former president.

The department did not make any public statements on the day of the search. The former president publicly confirmed the search that evening, as is his right.

Copies of both the warrant and the F.B.I. property receipt was provided on the day of the search that evening to the former president's council, who was on site during the search.

The search warrant was authorized by a federal court on required finding of probable cause.  The property receipt is a document that federal law requires law enforcement agents to leave with property owner.

The department filed a motion to make public the warrant and receipt in light of the former president public confirmation of the search, the surrounding circumstances, and the substantial public interest in this matter.

Much of our work is by necessity conducted out of the public eye. We do that to protect the constitutional rights of all Americans and to protect the integrity of our investigations

I personally approved the decision to seek a search warrant in this matter.

Watch the full video.

https://www.youtube.com/watch?v=aK
rJiynjd-E


A federal judge unsealed the search
warrant.  It identifies three federal crimes
that the Justice Department is looking at
as part of its investigation:


violations of the Espionage Act

obstruction of justice

criminal handling of government records


https://www.cnn.com/2022/08/12/poli
tics/search-warrant-receipt-trump-fbi-
maralago-key-
lines/index.html?utm_source=twCNNp
&utm_medium=social&utm_content=2
022-08-
12T22%3A33%3A07&utm_term=link

Eric Snowden exiled in Russia for violating the Espionage Act.

Part One

https://www.youtube.com/watch?v=kaUemcqIQ-k

Part 2

https://www.youtube.com/watch?v=rs2iN0oVdt4

# Michael Cohen

After admitting to campaign finance violations, tax evasion, and lying to Congress, Cohen was sentenced to three years in prison.

In 2019, Michael Cohen, the former lawyer and fixer for President Donald Trump, testified before the House Oversight Committee.

Excerpts from this hearing have since played a pivotal role in the indictment of a former president after leaving office. An intense exchange of rhetorical pyrotechnics marked the hearing.

The chairman of the committee, Rep. Elijah Cummings, a Democrat from

Maryland, made a pointed reference to Republicans during the hearing, alleging that members of the GOP on his panel were protecting President Trump.

"Ladies and gentlemen, the days of this committee protecting the president at all costs are over. They're over."

Jim Jordan: "This is the first time a convicted perjurer has been brought back to be a star witness."

Cohen's opening statement: "I am ashamed because I know what Mr. Trump is. He is a racist. He is a con man. He is a cheat."

"Mr. Trump is an enigma. He is complicated, as am I. He has both good and bad, as do we all," Cohen said. "But the bad far outweighs the good, and since taking office, he has become the worst version of himself. He is capable of behaving kindly, but he is not kind. He is capable of committing acts of generosity, but he is not generous. He is capable of being loyal, but he is fundamentally disloyal."

Cohen said Donald Trump, the candidate, was aware of a substantial email release that could prove detrimental to Hillary Clinton's chances of winning the election.

"Trump knew from Roger Stone in advance about the WikiLeaks drop of emails."

Rep. Jim Jordan: Cohen's remorse is minimal, his instinct to blame others is strong.

Cohen replied, "I said I plead guilty and I take responsibility for my actions ... Shame on you, Mr. Jordan."

Rep. Paul Gosar, R-Ariz: You are a "disgraced lawyer" No one should believe a word you say and taunted Cohen with, "Liar, liar, pants on fire."

Comer, a Republican Representative from Kentucky, inquired of Cohen, "If Trump is a cheat, then what are you?"

Cohen said, "A fool."

Cohen said that one of his greatest regrets was deceiving Melania Trump and concealing President Trump's supposed affair with pornographic actress Stormy Daniels. Cohen expressed remorse, stating, "Lying to the first lady is one of my biggest regrets. She is a kind, good person. I respect her greatly — and she did not deserve that."

After being bombarded with aggressive inquiries from Republican members, Cohen asked, in return, why is it that there are no questions regarding the President?

"I find it interesting that not one question from you today has been about Mr. Trump. That's why I thought I was coming today."

Rep. Jackie Speier, D-Californa:  "How many times did Mr. Trump ask you to threaten an individual or entity on his behalf 50, 100, 200, or 500 times?

Cohen said, "500 times."

Cohen's final statement proved to be true. Under the Trump administration, there will never be a peaceful transition of power...

"Indeed, given my experience working for Mr. Trump, I fear that if he loses the election in 2020 that there will never be a peaceful transition of power.  This is why I agreed to appear before you today."

Read the full testimony before the
House of Representatives Committee on
Oversight and Reform.

https://www.congress.gov/116/chrg/C
HRG-116hhrg35230/CHRG-
116hhrg35230.pdf

# Taken Down by a Porn Star

New York Investigation Targets Trump's Hush Money to Stormy Daniels; Cohen Testimony Implicates Ex-President.

Trump says he will be arrested on Tuesday, referring to himself (in 3rd person) says, "The leading Republican candidate and former president of the United States will be arrested. I'm completely innocent and did nothing wrong."

He continued, "If the Democrats can do this to President Trump, they can do it to you."

"WE MUST SAVE AMERICA! PROTEST, PROTEST, PROTEST!!!"

Trump is facing an investigation by New York District Attorney Alvin Bragg into whether his payments to adult film actress Stormy Daniels violated state election and document laws and whether they should be considered an illegal campaign expense.

If Bragg finds evidence of wrongdoing, Trump could be charged and potentially face jail time in New York.

In a statement, Cohen said, "At the end of the day, Donald Trump needs to be held accountable for his dirty deeds, if in fact, that's the way that the facts play out."

The investigation into Trump's payments to Daniels is part of a wider probe by Bragg's office into the Trump Organization's financial dealings. Bragg has indicated that he intends to take a hard line on white collar crime and corruption, which could spell trouble for the former president and his associates.

Trump called the Porn Star Stormy Daniels "Horseface" while President. Now it seems she will have the last word.

Meet Stormy Daniels

https://www.youtube.com/watch?v=gzCXdkFN3mQ

Trump, as President, derides and insults Stormy Daniels

https://www.youtube.com/watch?v=RXSHr-uyOkE&t=117s

Trump's life-long record would make an indictment unsurprising, Rachel Maddow explains.

https://www.youtube.com/watch?v=0t0qQ6aES8

# Why Waco, Texas?

Charles Manson, Jim Jones, and David Koresh were cult leaders. Don the Con Bat Shit Crazy the Former Guy, held a rally in Waco, Texas, home of the Branch Davidians, to recruit his next batch of devil worshipers amid potential indictment.

There is no coincidence that Trump held a rally in Waco, Texas, for his 2024 presidential campaign,  on the 30th Anniversary of the demise of the Cult Branch Davidians.

On February 28, 1993, a raid was conducted by the Bureau of Alcohol, Tobacco, and Firearms (ATF) on the Branch Davidian compound in Waco, Texas. This event marked the beginning

of a 51-day standoff between the federal
government and the religious group,
which ultimately ended in a tragic fire
and the deaths of over 70 people.

The Branch Davidians were a religious
group that was led by David Koresh, a
self-proclaimed messiah who claimed to
have a special relationship with God.
The group had been under the scrutiny
of law enforcement for several years, due
to reports of illegal firearms and
allegations of child abuse.

On the day of the raid, the ATF had
planned to execute a search warrant on
the compound, looking for illegal
firearms. However, they were met with
resistance from the Branch Davidians,
who had been tipped off about the raid
beforehand. A firefight ensued, which

resulted in the deaths of four ATF agents and six Branch Davidians.

After the initial raid, the FBI took over the operation and a standoff began. Negotiations between the FBI and the Branch Davidians took place over the course of several weeks, but no agreement could be reached. Tensions continued to escalate, with the FBI eventually cutting off the compound's electricity and water supply.

On April 19, 1993, the standoff came to a tragic end when the FBI attempted to end the siege by using tear gas to force the Branch Davidians out of the compound. However, a fire broke out and quickly engulfed the entire building.

In total, 76 Branch Davidians, including Koresh, died in the fire. Among the dead were 25 children, who were among the youngest members of the group.

The events at Waco, Texas, have been the subject of much controversy and debate over the years. Some people believe that the federal government was too aggressive in its tactics, and that the raid and subsequent standoff were unnecessary. Others argue that the Branch Davidians were a dangerous cult that posed a threat to society, and that the government was justified in its actions.

The tragedy at Waco also highlighted the dangers of cults and the power that charismatic leaders can hold over their followers. The Branch Davidians were a small group of people who were convinced to follow a man who claimed to be a messiah. This blind loyalty ultimately led to their deaths.

How does Timothy McVeigh, the Oklahoma Bomber relate to Waco?

Timothy McVeigh, who was responsible for the 1995 Oklahoma City bombing, was motivated in part by his anger towards the federal government's handling of the Waco siege. McVeigh believed that the government's actions at Waco were an egregious violation of civil liberties and that the deaths of the Branch Davidians were a result of excessive force.

McVeigh had actually visited the site of the Waco siege during the standoff and became convinced that the government was involved in a conspiracy to suppress individual rights. He saw the actions of the federal agents as an attack on American freedom and believed that the government was out of control.

McVeigh was so incensed by the events at Waco that he made it a key part of his anti-government ideology. In fact, he chose the date of the Oklahoma City bombing, April 19th, to coincide with the second anniversary of the Waco siege. This was meant as a symbolic gesture to draw attention to what he believed was an unjust and tyrannical government.

The Oklahoma City bombing was one of the deadliest acts of domestic terrorism in American history, resulting in the deaths of 168 people and injuring hundreds more. McVeigh's actions were driven in large part by his hatred of the federal government and his belief that it had become too powerful and corrupt.

In the aftermath of the Oklahoma City bombing, there was a renewed focus on the issue of domestic terrorism and the threat posed by extremist groups. The tragedy at Waco, which had already been a subject of controversy, took on new significance as it became clear that it had played a role in McVeigh's radicalization.

In conclusion, Timothy McVeigh's connection to the Waco siege underscores the lasting impact of this tragic event on American society. The deaths of the Branch Davidians and the government's handling of the siege were a catalyst for anti-government sentiment and played a key role in radicalizing one of the most notorious domestic terrorists in American history. The legacy of Waco continues to be felt to this day, both in terms of the ongoing debate over the role of government in religious groups and the ongoing threat of domestic terrorism.

As Timothy McVeigh put it, "Waco started this war."

Now Trump holds a rally in Waco, Texas, to keep the fires burning.

One rally supporter said God sent
Trump to her in a dream and said, "He is
a modern-day Cyrus. I sent him to save
the world."


People are blinded by their own reality.

# What is Truth?

What Is Truth

The reporter asks a MAGA supporter of Donald Trump, "What is it about him that brings you out here?"

MAGA Supporter: "Because when he was in there before, everything was wonderful. And when he left, everything went to hell."

Obviously, she is delusional.

Do you ever wish TRUTH would reveal ITSELF?

I'm looking for truth.

Where can I find it?

Do you have it?

Donald Trump, Rupert Murdoch, Fox News—they all say they have it. Preachers and politicians, Twitter and Facebook, too. So, tell me, do you have the truth? What is truth? Where can I find it?

Denzel Washington, when asked about fake news and the media, said,

"If you don't read the newspaper, you're uninformed. If you do read it, you're misinformed."

So, what do you do? What is the long-term effect of too much information?

"One of the effects is the need to be first, not even to be true anymore. The media has a great responsibility to tell the truth. Not just to be first, but to tell the truth. We live in a society now where it's just 'first—who cares, get it out there.' We don't care who it hurts. We don't care who it destroys. We don't care if it's true. Just say it. Sell it. Anything you practice, you'll get good at, even 'Bullshit.'"

So, what is truth? At its core, truth is the accurate representation of reality. It corresponds to facts, regardless of personal biases or opinions. In other words, truth is not a matter of belief but a matter of evidence.

However, it can be difficult to discern what is true and what is not. Social media has become a breeding ground for misinformation and fake news.

Even preachers, supposed sources of moral guidance and truth, are guilty of using their platforms to spread misinformation and intolerance. Just because someone says they are 'holier than thou' or a 'Christian Nationalist' doesn't mean they're not hypocrites. It doesn't matter if they quote scriptures—the devil can quote Bible verses too.

It's important to fact-check information and seek out multiple sources to corroborate or refute claims. Be aware of the algorithms that govern social media. They're designed to feed you information that locks you into your current beliefs.

So, once again, what is truth? Where is it?

In reality, truth is whatever you perceive it to be, whether it's right or wrong. Who is to tell you what is true?

Truth is the system. Whatever you're reading, seeing, hearing, and believing— that's true to you. And if it's not true, you will live with the consequences until you find out otherwise.

Truth is the horror of knowing.

# Conclusion

*A traitor of the United States of America,
appointed three Supreme Court Justices*

*Satan: "My work is almost done here."*

There is not a nation on the earth guilty
of

practices more shocking and bloodier
than are the

people of the United States, at this very
hour."

—Frederick Douglass in 1852

And we know from the insurrection that America's institutions were corrupt, and when the GOP Declared the Jan. 6 Attack 'Legitimate Political Discourse', we know now that America is sick.

Martin Luther King wrote, "While the question of who killed President Kennedy is important, the question of what killed him is more important." Racial hatred and the same is true for what made people attack the Capitol on Jan 6.

Our country is in grave danger. Not from a foreign enemy or a deadly pandemic but from Donald J Trump and his band of thugs. They have infiltrated every level of our institutions and destroyed our country from within.

Public hearings have revealed shocking evidence of Trump's conspiracy to overturn the government.

Will Donald Trump and his co-conspirators be held accountable and go to prison for their crimes?

Lawrence O'Donnell sees it differently. Trump is 76 years old and will likely spend the rest of his life as a defendant, facing legal exposure on multiple fronts. These legal battles will go on for 20 years, and he will end up in poor health and penniless.

Lawrence makes a very good point here.

https://www.youtube.com/watch?v=lcnsBjLviIA

Kellyanne Conway said in her book that Trump offered her an unsolicited pardon during the last days of his presidency and that during a discussion on pardons and clemency, Trump asked her, "Do you want one?" When she asked why Trump said, "Because they go after everyone, honey."

So, do you really want to know if Donald Trump and his conspirators, allies, children, senators, state and federal elected officials will all go to prison for their seditious and treasonous crimes to overthrow the government of the United States of America?

Now, if Donald Trump casually offered a pardon to Kellyanne Conway as if he was shopping for a loaf of bread, you can bet there's a 99.9% chance that he gave blanket pardons to each of his conspirators before he left the White House.

Gerald Ford on September 8, 1974, granted a full and unconditional pardon to Richard Nixon, his predecessor, for any crimes that he might have committed against the United States as president.

Oh, and Donald Trump, he would be dumber than dumb if he didn't issue an unconditional pardon to himself. No law prevents him from doing so.

Many legal experts say whatever happens, it won't keep Trump from running for President. He can run from jail--Eugene Debs ran for President from prison in 1920, and there's no law to prevent it from happening again, and the Secret Service will protect him at taxpayers' expense.

Well, there is something more ominous going on here.

Are we to believe this is the end, the devil wins the war between Good & Evil, and the villain walks away mocking God?

Is that what we should believe?

I should say not. Trump is half senile and half dead.

Although we live on a Dark Planet
where lies have seemingly overtaken the
Truth,  the Evil Doers wait on their
Comeuppance. They know who they are.


"Vengeance is mine!" sayeth the Lord.


The book continues...

# Revelation

*"But stay awake at all times, praying that you may have*

*strength to escape all these things that are going to take*

*place, and to stand before the Son of Man."*
*Luke 11:36*

I'm writing this for all the people that feel sad. People aren't nice, life is full of strife, make you feel like giving up, and say there is no hope. People hating, lying, cheating, mass shootings, corrupt politicians, and crooked preachers, things are worse than Sodom and Gomorrah. In times like these, you have to turn to the "Good Book" for answers.

Tell us, Lord, what will be a sign of your coming and the end of all the chaos and evil on earth.

Then the Lord said, "The outcry against Sodom and Gomorrah is so great and their sin so grievous that I will go down and see if what they have done is as bad as the outcry that has reached me. If not, I will know."

 The men turned away and went toward Sodom, but Abraham remained standing before the Lord.  Then Abraham approached him and said: "Will you sweep away the righteous with the wicked?

What if there are fifty righteous people in the city? Will you really sweep it away and not spare the place for the sake of the fifty righteous people in it? Far be it from you to do such a thing—to kill the righteous with the wicked, treating the righteous and the wicked alike. Far be it from you! Will not the Judge of all the earth do right?"

The Lord said, "If I find fifty righteous people in the city of Sodom, I will spare the whole place for their sake."

Then Abraham spoke up again: "Now that I have been so bold as to speak to the Lord, though I am nothing but dust and ashes, what if the number of the righteous is five less than fifty? Will you destroy the whole city for lack of five people?"

"If I find forty-five there," he said, "I will not destroy it."

Once again he spoke to him, "What if only forty are found there?"

He said, "For the sake of forty, I will not do it."

Then he said, "May the Lord not be angry, but let me speak. What if only thirty can be found there?"

He answered, "I will not do it if I find thirty there."

Abraham said, "Now that I have been so bold as to speak to the Lord, what if only twenty can be found there?"

He said, "For the sake of twenty, I will not destroy it."

Then he said, "May the Lord not be angry, but let me speak just once more. What if only ten can be found there?"

He answered, "For the sake of ten, I will not destroy it."

When the Lord had finished speaking with Abraham, he left, and Abraham returned home.

And there will be signs in sun and moon and stars, and on the earth distress of nations in perplexity because of the roaring of the sea and the waves, people fainting with fear and with foreboding of what is coming on the world.

For the powers of the heavens will be shaken.

But the day of the Lord will come like a thief, and then the heavens will pass away with a roar, and the heavenly bodies will be burned up and dissolved, and the earth and the works that are done on it will be exposed.

Then I saw an angel coming down from heaven, holding in his hand the key to the bottomless pit and a great chain.

And he seized the dragon, that ancient serpent, who is the devil and Satan, and bound him for a thousand years, and threw him into the pit, and shut it and sealed it over him, so that he might not deceive the nations any longer, until the thousand years were ended.

After that he must be released for a little while.

Then I saw thrones, and seated on them were those to whom the authority to judge was committed.

Also, I saw the souls of those who had been beheaded for the testimony of Jesus and for the word of God, and those who had not worshiped the beast or its image and had not received its mark on their foreheads or their hands.

They came to life and reigned with Christ for a thousand years.

The rest of the dead did not come to life until the thousand years were ended. This is the first resurrection. ...

Blessed is the one who reads aloud the words of this prophecy, and blessed are those who hear, and who keep what is written in it, for the time is near.

# Afterword

*America will fall without a shot being fired.*

*It will fall from within. Soviet leader, Nikita Khrushchev*

When a reporter asked Joe Biden, what was the motivation behind the J6 attack, he flatly replied, "White supremacy." It is a poison in America."

Judge Michael J Luttig said this to the Jan 6 Committee Public Hearing. "January 6 was but the next, foreseeable battle in a war that had been raging in America for years, though that day was the most consequential battle of that war even to date.

In fact, January 6 was a separate war unto itself, a war for America's democracy, a war irresponsibly instigated and prosecuted by the former president, his political party allies, and his supporters. Both wars are raging to this day."

—

We are at a "Pressure Point" where things are boiling over, and the very laws that were to provide equal justice for all have been exposed.  The sheets have been thrown back for everyone to see, and we found the Statue of Liberty naked beyond belief, and the Declaration of Independence, written by Thomas Jefferson, was "Full of deceit."

"We hold these truths to be self-evident, that all men are created equal, that they

are endowed by their Creator with certain unalienable Rights, that among
..."

The laws were never meant to be created equal with certain unalienable Rights. Instead, they were artfully made to protect the wealthy, their families, lawmakers, politicians, and the descendants of plantation owners that killed and publicly WHIPPED, BEAT, and LYNCHED black people while their children looked on.  And made white Americans believe that black people were savages and the White race was superior and passed this belief down through generations.

The KKK, White Supremacist groups, Proud Boys, Oath Keepers, and racist people have been waiting on their leader

Archie Bunker's grandson to arrive … the Antichrist with his racist MAGA message… Make America Great Again. Translation: Make America White Again.

But now, a different kind of war is going on that is not just waged against blacks.

It is a war against all Americans.

The three branches of government, the legislative, executive, and judicial, whose powers are vested by the U.S. Constitution in the Congress, the President, and the Federal courts, respectively—all are compromised.

Everyone can see the corrupt acts of Donald Trump and his Republican allies and supporters in plain sight.

When Donald Trump said, "I could tell a voter to kill someone on 5<sup>th</sup> Ave, and I wouldn't lose any voters," he knew he had a cult.  You saw the Jan 6 videos where his supporters said we traveled from all over the country to fight and lay down our lives for Donald Trump. "I'm willing to die, lay down my life for him… this is the least I can do… for everything that Trump has done for us and this country."


But they are poor, and their "financial status" hasn't changed in the four years he was president.


So, what kind of magic does Trump have on these people to make them act like evil demonic beings?

Lyndon B Johnson was asked why poor, white Republicans repeatedly vote against their own best interests, and he said, "If you can convince the lowest white man, he's better than the best colored man, he won't know you're picking his pocket. Hell, give him someone to look down on, and he'll empty his pockets for you."

Donald Trump said, "I love the poorly educated." Because they have been poor all their lives, they don't have anything and don't expect to have anything, now or in the future, but in their minds, at least they are not slaves or illegal aliens trying to cross the border (land that America stole).

So, when Donald Trump called Mexicans criminals, drug dealers, rapists, and killers and banned Muslims from coming into the country, poor whites felt superior and had "social status," I'm White.

*Under Trump, the wealthiest got tax cuts, the wall was never finished, and that's it!*

They don't care that Donald Trump is a cheat, a liar, and grifted millions of dollars on the Big Lie. Donald Trump is who they are.  They are him. That's how they justify their existence and are willing to die to prove it.

The Constitution is rigged, and the hagiarchy is stacked at the bottom (poor whites), working- class whites in the middle, and the wealthy at the top—and racist bigots that have infiltrated the institutions on the local, state, and federal levels.  And today, they are no longer covert about it.

A day after the Supreme Court overturned Roe vs. Wade and sent the country in turmoil, Republican Sen. John Cornyn commented on top of former President Barack Obama's tweet that denounced the Roe v. Wade decision.

Cornyn's tweet read, "Now do Plessy vs. Ferguson/Brown vs. Board of Education."

In other words, now overturn the 1954 SCOTUS ruling about segregation and let the states decide-- and Make America White Again.

<u>https://twitter.com/JohnCornyn/status/1540689961040482306</u>

When Benjamin Franklin was asked, "What do we have, a republic or a monarchy?"

Franklin replied, 'A republic if you can keep it.'

He knew the system would not last.  It took 233 years to unravel.

So, what can we do to save democracy? America is a sinking ship, and there is no fixing it.

"America is too great to fail."

I can assure you she is not. The Capitol is breached, the institutions are broken, and there is no "Truth" in the land … and no accountability. The make-shift gallows and the "Hang Mike Pence" chant should echo in your ears. It's too late.

"That is preposterous."

They said the very same thing in the movie  Titanic.

"God himself couldn't sink this ship."

"But the ship can't sink."  She's made of iron, sir. I assure you she can, and she will.

What's going on in the world today, there is no stopping it.

The Doomsday Clock remains at 100 seconds to midnight in 2022—the closest ever to apocalypse.

The farthest the clock has been from midnight was 17 minutes. That was in 1991.

And now … Armageddon, the last battle between good and evil before the Day of Judgment.

Please, God, have mercy. We've made a mess of things.

https://www.youtube.com/watch?v=-hsNZXe3r50

# Acknowledgements

*"You must be bold, brave,
and courageous and find a
way... to get in good trouble."* -John Lewis

I hope with this book that I found good trouble and took you places where you've never been. And I hope you will further your research into our country's past because that's the only way to understand the trouble we're in.

Lying is in vogue now, and when it leads to crime and goes unpunished, the world is a treacherous place.

A report says, '50% of devoted
Republicans would run off the cliff for
Trump they're all in,' another 20% wants
to push him off the cliff and that
number is growing. And there's 30% that
wants him to win."

I want to thank the Creator of Heaven
and Earth, Yahweh, for making me a
vessel to tell the story of Good and Evil.

And you, Dear God, are the real author,
the beginning, the finisher, and the end.

I also would like to thank my coauthor
Taylor Green for her research, expertise,
and unique writing skills that blended in
with mine.

And to you, the reader. Thank you for spending your time with us. You could have been anywhere, but you chose to be here.  Thank you.


P.S. If you haven't read Fallen Hero, book 1, jump over to Amazon and grab a copy, and while you're there, don't forget to write a review. And in case you didn't know, I've written 31 books, and this is my 4th book with Taylor Green. So, check out How to Cope with Intense Drama (similar to Glass Castle.)

# More Books by M LeMont

See authors page on Amazon

How To Cope with Intense Drama

Harry's Love Letters

Shh! Kiss Me Baby

M LeMont Caught Up What's Done In The Dark Comes To Light

<u>Hot trailer over 2,000 views</u>

HTG100K  Dare 2B GR8 Series

Book 1:  <u>How To Use Twitter: From Cradle To Grave</u>

Book 2: <u>How To Gain 100,000 Twitter Followers, Secrets Revealed An Expert</u>

Book 3: <u>Write Like You're Already Famous</u>

Shorter Sampling Version

<u>The Twitter Secret Key Revealed</u>

# Further Reading

Why Is It So Hard to Hold the Police Accountable?

https://youtu.be/kbR1lTk4N1A

The Trump Effect: New Study White America

https://www.nbcnews.com/think/amp/ncna877886

Many of the United States' most famous buildings were built by enslaved African Americans, including the White House and the US Capitol.

https://www.businessinsider.com/american-landmarks-that-were-built-by-slaves-2019-9

Plessy vs Ferguson Board of Education

https://www.wfaa.com/article/news/politics/john-cornyn-tweet-plessy-v-ferguson-brown-v-board-of-education/287-261b776b-65e5-4578-8f88-e49156cd2148

Isn't the Republicans the party that freed the slaves? Yes, but NOT these Republicans.

https://www.cnn.com/2020/08/27/politics/what-matters-august-26/index.html

John Eastman Emails reveal conspiracy to overturn the 2020 election.

https://newrepublic.com/article/166475/john-eastman-january-6-emails

Edward Snowden Interview

https://www.youtube.com/watch?v=e9yK1QndJSM

The British confronting their past and tearing down statues of former slave owners.

https://youtube.com/watch?v=rd_0zSlX5XM

Pardons, Blanket Pardons, Secret Pardons, Pocket Pardons

https://www.youtube.com/watch?v=18Afrdgq5gc

Trump's Pardon Abuses

https://www.politico.com/news/magazine/2022/06/22/trump-pardon-abuse-00041372

The judge that Mike Pence called for advice before certifying the electoral votes https://www.politico.com/news/2022/02/18/former-judge-beat-trump-january-6-00010056

How Former Judge Michael Luttig used
Twitter to save the day for Mike Pence

https://www.cnn.com/2022/02/20/poli
tics/judge-michael-luttig-pence-
tweet/index.html

Luttig Full Jan 6 Statement

https://www.politico.com/news/2022/
06/16/j-michael-luttig-opening-
statement-jan-6-hearing-00040255

Day 1 Public Hearing


https://www.youtube.com/watch?v=Ui
L2inz487U


Day 2: Public Hearing


https://www.youtube.com/watch?v=jbl
C2Ooog2U

## Day 3: Public Hearing

https://www.youtube.com/watch?v=7u4ocGJ9ZXI

## Day 4: Public Hearing

https://www.youtube.com/watch?v=YZPBWZcr-vw

## Day 5: Public Hearing

https://www.youtube.com/watch?v=8eNhqobJl_E

# Day 6: Cassidy Hutchinson, Star Witness, full testimony

https://www.youtube.com/watch?v=hSNBe-Wt6Q4

# Day 7: Public Hearing

https://www.youtube.com/watch?v=spJR5Y5_f4c

# Day 8: Public Hearing

https://www.youtube.com/watch?v=48
HH4LVn07g&t=1434s


Many of the United States' most famous
buildings were built by enslaved African
Americans, including the White House
and the US Capitol.


https://www.businessinsider.com/ameri
can-landmarks-that-were-built-by-slaves-
2019-9


Plessy vs Ferguson Board of Education


https://www.wfaa.com/article/news/po
litics/john-cornyn-tweet-plessy-v-
ferguson-brown-v-board-of-
education/287-261b776b-65e5-4578-
8f88-e49156cd2148

Full List of Fake Electors

https://www.azmirror.com/2022/06/29/updated-trumps-fake-electors-heres-the-full-list/

A vivid explanation on poor people and Social Capital.

https://twitter.com/MARCIAN2003/status/1536698462548410369

https://democracyrebooted.com/our-stolen-minds/

https://www.msnbc.com/msnbc/lyndon-johnson-civil-rights-racism-msna305591


Watergate Public hearings. John Dean, Star Witness Part 1


https://www.youtube.com/watch?v=UBHZ068Mwbg


Part 2  Watergate Hearings

https://www.youtube.com/watch?v=rE4jN8FuILE

Part 3 Watergate Hearings

https://www.youtube.com/watch?v=Mz1JPG5lR3s

Part 4 Watergate Hearings

https://www.youtube.com/watch?v=Yf5mxto8qws

Part 5 Watergate Hearings

https://www.youtube.com/watch?v=-b9995Y3XC8

Lyndon Johnson was Civil Rights Hero.
But he was also a racist.

https://www.msnbc.com/msnbc/lyndon-johnson-civil-rights-racism-msna305591

# Trump Farewell Address

Trump Gives Farewell Address, Urges Country To 'Pray' For Biden Administration

https://www.youtube.com/watch?v=W3XtYw_fXZE

My fellow Americans: Four years ago, we launched a great national effort to rebuild our country, to renew its spirit, and to restore the allegiance of this government to its citizens.  In short, we embarked on a mission to make America great again— for all Americans.

As I conclude my term as the 45th President of the United States, I stand

before you truly proud of what we have
achieved together.  We did what we
came here to do—and so much more.

This week, we inaugurate a new
administration and pray for its success in
keeping America safe and prosperous.
We extend our best wishes, and we also
want them to have luck—a very
important word.

I'd like to begin by thanking just a few of
the amazing people who made our
remarkable journey possible.

First, let me express my overwhelming
gratitude for the love and support of our
spectacular First Lady, Melania.  Let me
also share my deepest appreciation to my
daughter Ivanka, my son-in-law Jared,

and to Barron, Don, Eric, Tiffany, and Lara.  You fill my world with light and with joy.

I also want to thank Vice President Mike Pence, his wonderful wife Karen, and the entire Pence family.

Thank you as well to my Chief of Staff, Mark Meadows; the dedicated members of the White House Staff and the Cabinet; and all the incredible people across our administration who poured out their heart and soul to fight for America.

I also want to take a moment to thank a truly exceptional group of people: the United States Secret Service.  My family and I will forever be in your debt.

My profound gratitude as well to everyone in the White House Military Office, the teams of Marine One and Air Force One, every member of the Armed Forces, and state and local law enforcement all across our country.

Most of all, I want to thank the American people. To serve as your President has been an honor beyond description. Thank you for this extraordinary privilege. And that's what it is—a great privilege and a great honor.

We must never forget that while Americans will always have our disagreements, we are a nation of incredible, decent, faithful, and peace-loving citizens who all want our country to thrive and flourish and be very, very successful and good.  We are a truly magnificent nation.

All Americans were horrified by the assault on our Capitol.  Political violence is an attack on everything we cherish as Americans.  It can never be tolerated.

Now more than ever, we must unify around our shared values and rise above the partisan rancor, and forge our common destiny.

Four years ago, I came to Washington as the only true outsider ever to win the presidency.  I had not spent my career as a politician, but as a builder looking at open skylines and imagining infinite possibilities.

I ran for President because I knew there were towering new summits for America just waiting to be scaled.  I knew the potential for our nation was boundless as long as we put America first.

So I left behind my former life and stepped into a very difficult arena, but an arena nevertheless, with all sorts of potential if properly done.  America had given me so much, and I wanted to give something back.

Together with millions of hardworking patriots across this land, we built the greatest political movement in the history of our country.

We also built the greatest economy in the history of the world.  It was about

"America First" because we all wanted to make America great again. We restored the principle that a nation exists to serve its citizens.

Our agenda was not about right or left, it wasn't about Republican or Democrat, but about the good of a nation, and that means the whole nation.

With the support and prayers of the American people, we achieved more than anyone thought possible. Nobody thought we could even come close.

We passed the largest package of tax cuts and reforms in American history. We slashed more job-killing regulations than any administration had ever done before.

We fixed our broken trade deals, withdrew from the horrible Trans-Pacific Partnership and the impossible Paris Climate Accord, renegotiated the one-sided South Korea deal, and we replaced NAFTA with the groundbreaking USMCA—that's Mexico and Canada—a deal that's worked out very, very well.

Also, and very importantly, we imposed historic and monumental tariffs on China; made a great new deal with China.  But before the ink was even dry, we and the whole world got hit with the China virus.

Our trade relationship was rapidly changing, billions and billions of dollars were pouring into the U.S., but the virus forced us to go in a different direction.

The whole world suffered, but America outperformed other countries economically because of our incredible economy and the economy that we built. Without the foundations and footings, it wouldn't have worked out this way.

We wouldn't have some of the best numbers we've ever had.

We also unlocked our energy resources and became the world's number-one producer of oil and natural gas by far. Powered by these policies, we built the greatest economy in the history of the world.

We reignited America's job creation and achieved record-low unemployment for African Americans, Hispanic Americans,

Asian Americans, women—almost everyone.

Incomes soared, wages boomed, the American Dream was restored, and millions were lifted from poverty in just a few short years.  It was a miracle.

The stock market set one record after another, with 148 stock market highs' during this short period of time, and boosted the retirements and pensions of hardworking citizens all across our nation.  401(k)s are at a level they've never been at before.  We've never seen numbers like we've seen, and that's before the pandemic and after the pandemic.

We rebuilt the American manufacturing base, opened up thousands of new factories, and brought back the beautiful phrase: "Made in the USA."

To make life better for working families, we doubled the child tax credit and signed the largest-ever expansion of funding for childcare and development. We joined with the private sector to secure commitments to train more than 16 million American workers for the jobs of tomorrow.

When our nation was hit with the terrible pandemic, we produced not one, but two vaccines with record-breaking speed, and more will quickly follow. They said it couldn't be done but we did it. They call it a "medical miracle," and that's what they're calling it right now: a "medical miracle."

Another administration would have taken 3, 4, 5, maybe even up to 10 years to develop a vaccine.  We did in nine months.

We grieve for every life lost, and we pledge in their memory to wipe out this horrible pandemic once and for all.

When the virus took its brutal toll on the world's economy, we launched the fastest economic recovery our country has ever seen.  We passed nearly $4 trillion in economic relief, saved or supported over 50 million jobs, and slashed the unemployment rate in half.

These are numbers that our country has never seen before.

We created choice and transparency in healthcare, stood up to big pharma in so many ways, but especially in our effort to get favored-nations clauses added, which will give us the lowest prescription drug prices anywhere in the world.

We passed VA Choice, VA Accountability, Right to Try, and landmark criminal justice reform.

We confirmed three new justices of the United States Supreme Court.  We appointed nearly 300 federal judges to interpret our Constitution as written.

For years, the American people pleaded with Washington to finally secure the nation's borders.  I am pleased to say we answered that plea and achieved the most secure border in U.S. history.  We have given our brave border agents and heroic ICE officers the tools they need to do their jobs better than they have ever done before, and to enforce our laws and keep America safe.

We proudly leave the next administration with the strongest and most robust border security measures ever put into place.  This includes historic agreements with Mexico, Guatemala, Honduras, and El Salvador, along with more than 450 miles of powerful new wall.

We restored American strength at home and American leadership abroad.  The

world respects us again.  Please don't
lose that respect.

We reclaimed our sovereignty by
standing up for America at the United
Nations and withdrawing from the one-
sided global deals that never served our
interests.  And NATO countries are now
paying hundreds of billions of dollars
more than when I arrived just a few
years ago.  It was very unfair.  We were
paying the cost for the world.  Now the
world is helping us.

And perhaps most importantly of all,
with nearly $3 trillion, we fully rebuilt the
American military—all made in the USA.
We launched the first new branch of the
United States Armed Forces in 75 years:
the Space Force.  And last spring, I
stood at Kennedy Space Center in

Florida and watched as American astronauts returned to space on American rockets for the first time in many, many years.

We revitalized our alliances and rallied the nations of the world to stand up to China like never before.

We obliterated the ISIS caliphate and ended the wretched life of its founder and leader, al Baghdadi.  We stood up to the oppressive Iranian regime and killed the world's top terrorist, Iranian butcher Qasem Soleimani.

We recognized Jerusalem as the capital of Israel and recognized Israeli sovereignty over the Golan Heights.

As a result of our bold diplomacy and principled realism, we achieved a series of historic peace deals in the Middle East.  Nobody believed it could happen. The Abraham Accords opened the doors to a future of peace and harmony, not violence and bloodshed.  It is the dawn of a new Middle East, and we are bringing our soldiers home.

I am especially proud to be the first President in decades who has started no new wars.

Above all, we have reasserted the sacred idea that, in America, the government answers to the people.  Our guiding light, our North Star, our unwavering conviction has been that we are here to serve the noble everyday citizens of America.  Our allegiance is not to the special interests, corporations, or global entities; it's to our children, our citizens, and to our nation itself.

As President, my top priority, my constant concern, has always been the best interests of American workers and American families.  I did not seek the easiest course; by far, it was actually the most difficult.  I did not seek the path that would get the least criticism.  I took on the tough battles, the hardest fights, the most difficult choices because that's what you elected me to do.  Your needs were my first and last unyielding focus.

This, I hope, will be our greatest legacy: Together, we put the American people back in charge of our country.  We restored self-government.  We restored the idea that in America no one is forgotten, because everyone matters and everyone has a voice. We fought for the principle that every citizen is entitled to equal dignity, equal treatment, and equal rights because we are all made equal by God. Everyone is entitled to be treated with respect, to have their voice heard, and to have their government listen. You are loyal to your country, and my administration was always loyal to you.

We worked to build a country in which every citizen could find a great job and support their wonderful families. We fought for the communities where every American could be safe and schools where every child could learn. We promoted a culture where our laws would be upheld, our heroes honored, our history preserved, and law-abiding citizens are never taken for granted. Americans should take tremendous satisfaction in all that we have achieved together.  It's incredible.

Now, as I leave the White House, I have been reflecting on the dangers that threaten the priceless inheritance we all share.  As the world's most powerful nation, America faces constant threats and challenges from abroad.  But the greatest danger we face is a loss of confidence in ourselves, a loss of confidence in our national greatness.  A nation is only as strong as its spirit.  We are only as dynamic as our pride.  We are only as vibrant as the faith that beats in the hearts of our people.

No nation can long thrive that loses faith in its own values, history, and heroes, for these are the very sources of our unity and our vitality.

What has always allowed America to prevail and triumph over the great challenges of the past has been an unyielding and unashamed conviction in the nobility of our country and its unique purpose in history. We must never lose this conviction. We must never forsake our belief in America.

The key to national greatness lies in sustaining and instilling our shared national identity. That means focusing on what we have in common: the heritage that we all share.

At the center of this heritage is also a robust belief in free expression, free speech, and open debate. Only if we forget who we are, and how we got here, could we ever allow political censorship and blacklisting to take place in America. It's not even thinkable. Shutting down free and open debate violates our core values and most enduring traditions.

In America, we don't insist on absolute conformity or enforce rigid orthodoxies and punitive speech codes. We just don't do that. America is not a timid nation of tame souls who need to be sheltered and protected from those with whom we disagree. That's not who we are. It will never be who we are.

For nearly 250 years, in the face of every challenge, Americans have always summoned our unmatched courage, confidence, and fierce independence. These are the miraculous traits that once led millions of everyday citizens to set out across a wild continent and carve out a new life in the great West.  It was the same profound love of our God-given freedom that willed our soldiers into battle and our astronauts into space.

As I think back on the past four years, one image rises in my mind above all others.  Whenever I traveled all along the motorcade route, there were thousands and thousands of people.  They came out with their families so that they could stand as we passed, and proudly wave our great American flag.  It never failed to deeply move me.  I knew that they did not just come out to show their support of me; they came out to show me their support and love for our country.

This is a republic of proud citizens who are united by our common conviction that America is the greatest nation in all of history.  We are, and must always be, a land of hope, of light, and of glory to all the world.  This is the precious inheritance that we must safeguard at every single turn.

For the past four years, I have worked to do just that.  From a great hall of Muslim leaders in Riyadh to a great square of Polish people in Warsaw; from the floor of the Korean Assembly to the podium at the United Nations General Assembly; and from the Forbidden City in Beijing to the shadow of Mount Rushmore, I fought for you, I fought for your family, I fought for our country.  Above all, I fought for America and all it stands for—and that is safe, strong, proud, and free.

Now, as I prepare to hand power over to a new administration at noon on Wednesday, I want you to know that the movement we started is only just beginning.  There's never been anything like it.  The belief that a nation must serve its citizens will not dwindle but instead only grow stronger by the day.

As long as the American people hold in their hearts deep and devoted love of country, then there is nothing that this nation cannot achieve.  Our communities will flourish.  Our people will be prosperous.  Our traditions will be cherished.  Our faith will be strong.  And our future will be brighter than ever before.

I go from this majestic place with a loyal and joyful heart, an optimistic spirit, and

a supreme confidence that for our
country and for our children, the best is
yet to come.

Thank you, and farewell.  God bless you.
God bless the United States of America.

The White House

Watch Full Video

https://www.youtube.com/watch?v=W
3XtYw_fXZE

# Reference Sources


*Richard Nixon Quotes Courtesy, Daniel Kurtzman*

*https://www.liveabout.com/richard-nixon-quotes-2733879*


Scriptures


https://www.openbible.info/topics/end_of_the_world


Luke 21:36, Revelation 1:3, 2 Timothy 3:1-5 2, Corinthians 4:4

Jones Speech I am God

http://jonestown.sdsu.edu/?page_id=30849

Jonestown

https://www.theatlantic.com/national/archive/2011/11/drinking-the-kool-aid-a-survivor-remembers-jim-jones/248723/

Notes—*Excerpt Jonestown



http://www.nytimes.com/1979/11/18/archives/jonestown-the-survivors-story-jonestown.html


The Bulletin of the Atomic Scientists.
The Doomsday Clock


Book-- Stamped (Racism, Antiracism, and You)

# Transcript (MeltDown)

543

*"Dead people … and we have many examples*
*filled out ballots made applications*
*and then voted*
*which is even worse in other words …*
*dead people went through a process*
*some of them been dead for 25 years.*
*Millions of votes cast illegally*
*in swing states alone."*

Witness Donald Trump, a dumb and stupid man who is the most powerful man in America.

A friendless man who ran for President as a hoax and won. A compulsive, unloved, narcissist, and lonely man who learned nothing from his first impeachment.

His only concern is for himself, TV ratings and staying in 'Power.

This is a man who has lived 74 lying and unconscionable years... and, who at this moment knows he's totally fucked!

https://www.youtube.com/watch?v=WP0ixjE7JIU

President Donald Trump: (00:00)

Thank you. This may be the most important speech I've ever made.

I want to provide an update on our ongoing efforts to expose the tremendous voter fraud and irregularities which took place during the ridiculously long November 3rd elections.

We used to have what was called, election day. Now we have election days, weeks, and months, and lots of bad things happened during this ridiculous period of time, especially when you have to prove almost nothing to exercise our greatest privilege, the right to vote.

As President, I have no higher duty than to defend the laws and the Constitution of the United States.

That is why I am determined to protect our election system, which is now under coordinated assault and siege.

President Donald Trump: (00:54)

For months, leading up to the Presidential election, we were warned that we should not declare a premature victory.

We were told repeatedly that it would take weeks if not, months, to determine the winner, to count the absentee ballots and to verify the results. My opponent was told to stay away from the election, don't campaign.

"We don't need you. We've got it. This election is done." In fact, they were acting like they already knew what the outcome was going to be. They had it covered and perhaps they did, very sadly for our country. It was all very, very strange. Within days after the election, we witnessed an orchestrated effort to anoint the winner even while many key states were still being counted.

President Donald Trump: (01:44)

The constitutional process must be allowed to continue. We're going to defend the honesty of the vote by ensuring that every legal ballot is counted and that no illegal ballot is counted.

This is not just about honoring the votes of 74 million Americans who voted for me, it's about ensuring that Americans can have faith in this election and in all future elections.

President Donald Trump: (02:12)

Today I will detail some of the shocking irregularities, abuses and fraud that had been revealed in recent weeks but before laying out just a small portion of the evidence we have uncovered, and we have so much evidence, I want to explain the corrupt mail-in balloting scheme that Democrats systematically put into place that allowed voting to be altered, especially in swing states, which they had to win.

They just didn't know that it was going to be that tough, because we were

leading in every swing state by so much,
far greater than they ever thought
possible.


While it has long been understood that
the Democrat political machine engages
in voter fraud from Detroit to
Philadelphia, to Milwaukee, Atlanta, so
many other places.

What changed this year was the Democrat party's relentless push to print and mail out tens of millions of ballots sent to unknown recipients with virtually no safeguards of any kind. This allowed fraud and abuse to occur in a scale never seen before.

Using the pandemic as a pretext, Democrat politicians and judges drastically changed election procedures just months, and in some cases, weeks before the election on the 3rd of November.

President Donald Trump: (03:45)

Very rarely were legislatures involved and constitutionally, they had to be involved, but very, very rarely, and you'll see that as we continue to file our suits, it's constitutionally, absolutely incorrect what took place, even from a legal standpoint. Many states, such as Nevada and California sent millions of live ballots to every person on their voter rolls whether those individuals had requested ballots or not, whether they were dead or alive, they got ballots.

Other states such as Minnesota, Michigan, and Wisconsin, instituted universal absentee balloting right in the middle of an election year, sending absentee ballot requests forms to all voters on all rolls. It didn't matter who they were.

This colossal expansion of mail-in voting opened the flood gates to massive fraud. It's a widely known fact that the voting rolls are packed with people who are not lawfully eligible to vote, including those who are deceased, have moved out of their state, and even our non-citizens of our country.

President Donald Trump: (05:05)

Beyond this, the records are riddled with errors, wrong addresses, duplicate entries, and many other issues.

This is not disputed. It has never been disputed. Dozens of counties in the key swing states have more registered voters on the rolls than they have voting age citizens, including 67 counties in Michigan.

All of this is evidence. In Wisconsin, the state's Board of Elections could not confirm the residency of more than 100,000 people, but repeatedly refused to remove those names from its voter rolls before the election.

They knew why, nobody else did. I knew why. They were illegal voters. It is a travesty that in the year 2020, we do not have any means of verifying the eligibility of those who cast ballots in an election and such an important election it is, or determining who they are, whether they live in the state or whether they're even American citizens. We have no idea.

President Donald Trump: (06:21)

We have an in all swing states major infractions or outright fraud, which is far more in numbers or votes then we need to overturn the results of a state.

In other words, in Wisconsin, as an example, where we were way up on election night, they ultimately had us miraculously losing by 20,000 votes.

I can show you right here, that Wisconsin, we're leading by a lot and then at 3:42 in the morning, there was this, it was a massive dump of votes, mostly Biden, almost all Biden. To this day, everyone's trying to figure out, "Where did it come from?"

But I went from leading by a lot, to losing by a little and that's right here.

That's at 3:42 in the morning, that's Wisconsin, a terrible thing, terrible, terrible thing.

President Donald Trump: (07:33)

But we will have far more, many times more than the 20,000 votes needed to overturn the state. If we are right about the fraud, Joe Biden can't be president.

We're talking about hundreds of thousands of votes.

We're talking about numbers like nobody has ever seen before.

Just as an example, in certain states, we'll be down by, let's say, 7,000 votes, but we'll find later on 20,000, 50,000, 100,00, 200,000 discrepancies or fraudulent votes, and that includes votes that went through when they were not allowed to be seen by Republican poll watchers, because the poll watchers were locked out of the building.

Or people that innocently came to vote on November 3rd, who were all excited about their vote, they were happy.

They were proud to be citizens of the United States of America, and they went up and they said, "I'd like to vote."

They were told that they can't vote. "I'm sorry," they were told, "I'm sorry. You've already voted by mail-in ballot. Congratulations. We received a ballot, so you can no longer vote."

President Donald Trump: (09:03)

They didn't know what to do. They had no one to complain to, most just left and said, "That's strange."

But many people complained and complained vehemently, and in a lot of cases, they filled out a provisional ballot, which was almost never used, but in virtually every case was a vote for Trump.

In other words, they went in to vote and they were told that they voted and they didn't vote.

They left and they felt horror and they lost respect for our system. This happened tens of thousands of times all over the country.

That's how desperate the Democrats were.

They would fill out ballots of people not even knowing if these people were going to show up. When they did show up, they said, "Sorry, you've already voted."

President Donald Trump: (10:07)

On top of everything else, we have a company that's very suspect. It's name is Dominion, with the turn of a dial or the change of a chip, you could press a button for Trump and the vote goes to Biden.

What kind of a system is this?

We have to go to paper, maybe it takes longer. But the only secure system is paper.

Not these systems that nobody understands, including in many cases, the people that run them. Although, unfortunately, I think they understand them far too well.

President Donald Trump: (10:46)

In one Michigan County, as an example, that used Dominion systems, they found that nearly 6,000 votes had been wrongly switched from Trump to Biden, and this is just the tip of the iceberg.

This is what we caught.

How many didn't we catch? Are there 100s of other examples throughout the country? Are there 1000s?

We just got lucky and they called it a glitch, but we found numerous glitches that evening. 96% of the company's political donations went to Democrats, not surprisingly.

Frankly, when you look at who's running the company, who's in charge, who owns it, which we don't know, where are the votes counted? Which we think are counted in foreign countries, not in the United States, Dominion is a disaster. Election authorities in Texas have repeatedly blocked the deployment of Dominion systems due to concerns about security vulnerabilities and the potential for errors and outright fraud.

Every district that uses Dominion systems must be carefully monitored and carefully investigated, but not only for the future.

President Donald Trump: (12:01)

Right now, we're worried about the present, and what went on with an election that we won without question.

Under my lead, the Republicans won almost every state house in the United States, which they weren't expected to do. We went up to 16 seats in the house. The numbers are still being tabulated, because there are nine seats that nobody really knows. They don't know.

Two weeks later, it's still under consideration, because it's a mess.

Republicans were supposed to lose many seats, and instead they won those seats in the house, and a very important election that's coming up will determine whether, or not we hold the Senate.

President Donald Trump: (12:59)

David Perdue and Kelly Leffler are two tremendous people. Unfortunately, in Georgia, they're using the same horrible dominion system, and it's already been out that, think of it, hundreds of thousands of absentee ballots have been requested.

You check it out who's requesting those ballots.

The difference is, it's one state, and we will have our eyes on it like nobody's ever watched anything before, because we have to win those two Senate seats.

The tremendous success we had in the House of Representatives, and the tremendous success we've had so far in the Senate, unexpected success all over the country, and right here in Washington.

President Donald Trump: (13:55)

It is statistically impossible that the person, me, that led the charge lost.

The greatest pollsters, the real pollsters, not the ones that had us down 17 points in Wisconsin when we actually won, or the ones that had us down four or five points in Florida, and we won by many points, or had us even, and down in Texas, and we won by a lot, not those pollsters, but real pollsters.

Pollsters that are fair, and honest said, "We can't understand a thing like this.

It's never happened before. You led the country to victory, and you were the only one that was lost. It's not possible."

President Donald Trump: (14:43)

The speaker of the house of a certain state said, "Sir, I expected to lose my seat, and instead, because of you, and because of that incredible charge, and all of those rallies, we had a tremendous victory, and everybody knows it.

You are much more popular than me, sir, except I got many more votes than you did, and it's impossible that that happened. There is something wrong."

I'll tell you what's wrong, voter fraud. Here's an example. This is Michigan. At

6:31 in the morning, a vote dump of 149,772 votes came in unexpectedly. We were winning by a lot. That batch was received in horror.

President Donald Trump: (15:44)

Nobody knows anything about it. By the way, there's your line.

This is one of many. Here's what is normal, and all of a sudden, look at that.

This is normal, normal.

Look even here, normal, and then boom, all of a sudden, I go from winning by a lot to losing a tight race.

It's corrupt. Detroit is corrupt. I have a lot of friends in Detroit. They know it, but Detroit is totally corrupt.

Look at this, look at this. That's at 6:31 in the morning, unexpectedly came in. In the recent recount in Georgia, which means nothing because they don't want to check signatures, and if you're not going to check signatures in Georgia, it doesn't work, but we have a secretary of state, and a governor who made it very difficult to check signatures.

President Donald Trump: (16:41)

Why? You'll have to ask them, but without a signature match, or a check, it doesn't matter.

They found thousands and thousands of votes that were out of whack, all against me.

This was during a recount that I didn't even think mattered. They found many thousands of votes, and that recount didn't matter.

The one that matters is the one that's going on now, that because of the fact it's so close, they had to by law give another recount, but the recount has to be a recount where they check the signatures. Otherwise, they're just checking the same dishonest thing. It won't matter.

President Donald Trump: (17:22)

In this case, the signatures on envelopes are the only thing that is relevant. We will compare the signature on the envelope to the signatures from past elections, and we will find that many thousands of people signed these ballots illegally.

The Democrats had this election rigged right from the beginning.

They used the pandemic, sometimes referred to as the China virus, where it originated as an excuse to mail out tens of millions of ballots, which ultimately led to a big part of the fraud, a fraud that the whole world is watching, and there is no one happier right now than China.

President Donald Trump: (18:10)

Many people received two, three and four ballots. They were sent to dead people by the thousands. In fact, dead people, and we have many examples filled out ballots, made applications, and then, voted, which is even worse.

In other words, dead people went through a process. Some have been dead for 25 years. Millions of votes were cast illegally in the swing states alone, and if that's the case, the results of the individual swing states must be overturned, and overturned immediately.

Some people say that's too far out, that's too harsh.

Well, does that mean we take a precedent, and we've just elected a president where the votes were fraudulent?

President Donald Trump: (19:01)

No, it means you have to turn over the election, and everybody knows without going much further, and they've seen the evidence, but they don't want to talk about it what a disaster this election was, a total catastrophe, but we're going to show it, and hopefully, the courts in particular, the Supreme Court of the United States will see it, and respectfully, hopefully, they will do what's right for our country, because our country can not live with this kind of an election.

We could say, let's go on to the next one, but no, we have to look also at our past. We can't let this happen.

President Donald Trump: (19:43)

Maybe you'll have a revote, but I don't think that's appropriate.

When those votes are corrupt, when
they're irregular, when they get caught,
they're terminated, and I very easily win.

In all states, I very easily win, the swing
states, just like I won them at 10 o'clock
in the evening, the evening of the
election.

We're not looking to show you 25 faulty
or fraudulent votes, which don't mean
anything, because it doesn't overturn the
state, or a fifty, or a hundred.

We're showing you hundreds of
thousands far more than we need, far
more than the margin, far more than the
law requires. We can show many times
what is necessary to win the state.

President Donald Trump: (20:34)

The media knows this, but they don't want to report it. In fact, they outright refuse to even cover it, because they know the result if they do. Even what I'm saying now will be demeaned and disparaged, but that's okay.

I just keep on going forward, because I'm representing 74 million people, and in fact, I'm also representing all of the people that didn't vote for me.

The mail-in voting scam is the latest part of their four-year effort to overturn the results of the 2016 election, and it's been like living in hell.

Our opponents have proven many times again and again, that they will say, and do anything to get back into power.

President Donald Trump: (21:28)

The corrupt forces who are registering dead voters and stuffing ballot boxes are the same people who have perpetrated one phony and fraudulent hoax after another. You've been watching it now for four years. These entrenched interests oppose our movement, because we put America first. They don't put America first, and we're returning power to you the American people.

They don't want America first; they only want power for themselves. They want to make money, that's why they don't want me as your president. I've been investigated from soon after I announced I was running for president.

When I immediately went to number one in the Republican primary polls, the investigations never stopped.

They went on for four years, and I won them all, I beat them all. Russia, Russia, Russia, the impeachment hoax, and so much more.

Robert Mueller spent $48 million of taxpayer money investigating me for two and a half years, issued over 2,800 subpoenas, executed nearly 500 search warrants, issued 230 orders for communications records, and conducted

500 witness interviews, all looking to take me down.

There was no collusion in the end, none whatsoever. Senator Marco Rubio, the head of the Senate Intelligence Committee stated, "The committee found no evidence that then candidate Donald Trump, or his campaign colluded with the Russian government." And, I thank Senator Rubio for that statement.

President Donald Trump: (23:22)

Now, I hear that these same people that failed to get me in Washington have sent every piece of information to New York, so that they can try to get me there. It's all been gone over, over and over again.

For $48 million you go through tax returns, you go through everything.

The New York attorney general, who recently ran for office campaigned without knowing me stating, "We will join with law enforcement and other attorneys general across this nation in removing this president from office." I never met her.

President Donald Trump: (24:03)

"It's important that everybody understands", she said, "that the days of Donald Trump are coming to an end." And all it's been is a big investigation in Washington and New York and any place else that can investigate because that's what they want to do.

They want to take not me, but us down. Then we can never let them do that. Everything has been looked at. A friend of mine, who's very smart, said, "You've probably seen more than anybody else.

You've probably been investigated more than anybody else. And for you to come out with a clean bill of health makes you probably the cleanest person in this country."

President Donald Trump: (24:48)

Some people in this administration, but fortunately not all have been beaten down and disparaged. They just disappeared. Nobody knows what happened to them. Why aren't they active?

Why aren't they involved? There's so much to be involved in. The corruption is so rampant. They just couldn't take it anymore.

They were threatened by Democrats with impeachment and horrible things were said about them. And they're good people. Even recently, the head of the GSA was hounded and harassed as she reported, like she has never been before.

What can I say? We caught Comey cold, we caught McCabe cold. We caught them all. We're still waiting for a report from a man named Durham, who I have never spoken to, and I have never met.

They can go after me before the election as much as they want, but unfortunately Mr. Durham didn't want to go after these people, or have anything to do with going after them before the election. So who knows if he is ever going to even do a report.

President Donald Trump: (26:11)

But if you look at the lies, and the leaks, and the illegal acts of behavior done by so many people, and their desire to hurt the president of the United States, something should happen.

The hardest thing I have to do is explain why nothing is happening with all of these people that got caught spying on my campaign.

It's never happened before and it should never happen again to a president of the United States. All you have to do is watch the hearings and see for yourself.

The evidence is overwhelming. The fraud that we've collected in recent weeks is overwhelming, having to do with our election.

Everyone is saying, " Wow, the evidence is overwhelming", when they get to see it. But really it's too late to change the course of an election. It's too late to change the outcome.

President Donald Trump: (27:11)

In fact, there is still plenty of time to certify the correct winner of the election and that's what we're fighting to do.

But no matter when it happens, when they see fraud, when they see false votes and when those votes number far more than is necessary, you can't let another person steal that election from you. All over the country, people are together in holding up signs, "Stop the steal."

To understand how we will challenge this fraud, it is important to know the problems with mail-in balloting. Pennsylvania, Michigan, Nevada, Georgia, Arizona, and most other states allowed anyone to get an absentee ballot and cast their vote without showing any ID.

The voting took place entirely on the honor system, no identification of any kind was required.

President Donald Trump: (28:11)

Most Americans would also be shocked to learn that no state in the country verifies United States citizenship as a condition for voting in federal elections.

This is a national disgrace. No other advanced country conducts elections this way.

Many European countries have instituted major restrictions on mail-in voting, specifically, because they recognize the nearly unlimited potential for fraud. Out of 42 European nations, all but two prohibit absentee ballots entirely for people who reside inside the country, or else they require those who need absentee ballots to show a very, very powerful ID.

President Donald Trump: (28:54)

Throughout the Democrat effort to dramatically expand mail-in voting, the Democrat party leaders were also, feverishly working to block measures, designed to protect against fraud, such as signature verification, residency verification, or voter ID. And citizenship confirmation was almost unthought of that we should ask for it. Can you believe this?

These are not the actions of people who want fair elections.

These are the actions of people who want to steal elections, who are willing to create fraud. The only conceivable reason why you would block common sense measures to verify legal eligibility for voting, is you are trying to encourage, enable, solicit, or carry out fraud.

President Donald Trump: (29:47)

It is important for Americans to understand that these destructive changes to our election laws were not a necessary response to the pandemic. The pandemic simply gave the Democrats an excuse to do what they have been trying to do for many, many years. In fact, the very first bill that house Democrats introduced when Nancy Pelosi became speaker, was it attempt to mandate universal mail-in voting and eliminate measures such as voter ID, which is so necessary. Dramatically eroding the integrity of our elections was the Democrats number one priority for a simple reason, they wanted to steal the 2020 presidential election.

All of the Democrat efforts to expand mail-in balloting laid the groundwork for the systematic and pervasive fraud that occurred in this election.

President Donald Trump: (30:41)

In Pennsylvania, large amounts of mail-in and absentee ballots were processed illegally. And in secret, in Philadelphia, in Allegheny counties, without our observers present. They were not allowed to be present. In fact, they weren't even allowed in the same room. They were thrown out of the building and they looked from outside in, but they had no way of even seeing, because there were no windows.

And the windows that were there were boarded up. Democrats even went to the Pennsylvania Supreme Court to block observers from receiving access.

There is only one possible reason that the corrupt Democrat political machine would oppose transparency during the vote counting. It's because they know they are hiding illegal activity. It's very simple.

President Donald Trump: (31:32)

This is an egregious, inexcusable.

And irreversible harm that stains the entire election, yet this unprecedented practice of excluding our observers, our vote watchers, as some people call them, occurred in Democrat run cities and key states all across the nation.

Here are just some of the additional facts that we've uncovered. Many voters all across Pennsylvania received two ballots in the mail, and many others received mail-in ballots for which they never applied.

So many get ballots, they didn't even know what they were for. And again, so many received more than one ballot. In some cases, more than two ballots. And they happened to be, for the most part, Democrats.

President Donald Trump: (32:22)

In Fayette County, Pennsylvania, multiple voters received ballots that were already filled out.

They didn't know what happened.

In Montgomery County, Pennsylvania, a poll watcher, overheard unregistered voters being told to return later to try to vote under a different name.

Tens of thousands of voters across Pennsylvania were treated differently based on whether they were

Republicans, or Democrats. Voters who submitted floored ballots in some Democrat precincts were notified and asked to fix their ballots, while Republican precincts, and in particular Republican voters, were not so notified which plainly violates the Equal Protection Clause of the United States Constitution. "If you are a Democrat, we're going to fix up your ballot. make sure it's perfect. If you are Republican, don't even talk about it."

President Donald Trump: (33:16)

In Michigan, a career employee of the city of Detroit, with the city workers, coaching voters to vote straight Democrat, while accompanying them to watch who they were voting for, violating the law and the sanctity of the secret ballot.

You can't do that. The same workers say she was instructed not to ask for any ID and not to attempt to validate any signatures. She was also told to illegally backdate ballots, many, many ballots, received after the deadline.

This is something that is so unconstitutional and she estimates that thousands and thousands of ballots were improperly backdated by her and many others.

President Donald Trump: (34:05)

Other witnesses in Detroit also saw our election officials counting batches of the same ballots many times, as well as illegally duplicating ballots. One observer testified to seeing boxes and boxes of ballots, all bearing the same signature. Another observer in Detroit gave sworn testimony that he saw countless and valid ballots that did not belong to properly registered voters and then witnessed election workers in Wayne County entering fake birth dates into the system, in order to illegally count them. Witnesses of science wore an affidavit, so in other words, you go to jail if you lie, testifying that after election officials announced the last absentee votes had been received, a batch of tens of thousands of ballots arrived, many without envelopes, all voting for Democrats.


President Donald Trump: (35:02)

In Wisconsin, a record number of voters were categorized as indefinitely confined. A status reserved for severely disabled individuals, also for the elderly that allow them to vote without showing ID. Last year, approximately 70,000 people claimed this status statewide. This year, the number miraculously was nearly 250,000 voters, after election officials in Milwaukee and Dane County, a couple of the most corrupt political places in our country, urged citizens to improperly register under this status. And register they did in levels that don't exist. In Wisconsin, there are approximately 70,000 absentee ballots that do not have matching ballot applications as required by law in Georgia, nine observers have testified to seeing countless irregular ballots without…

President Donald Trump: (36:03)

Testified to seeing countless irregular ballots without the creases or typical markings indicating that the ballots did not arrive in envelopes as required.

A poll watcher in Fulton County estimated that approximately 98% of the large number of unusually pristine ballots that she witnessed were for Biden. Highly unusual number.

In addition, thousands of uncounted ballots were discovered in Floyd, Fayette, and Walton counties weeks after the election, and these ballots were mostly from Trump voters. They weren't counted. They were from Trump voters.

President Donald Trump: (36:43)

In Detroit, everybody saw the tremendous conflict and the horrible way that the two Republican canvassers were treated so horribly because they wouldn't vote when they saw that 71% of the precincts didn't balance.

Also, there were more votes than there were voters. Think of that. You had more votes than you had voters.

That's an easy one to figure, and it's by the thousands.

In Arizona, in-person voters whose balanced produced error messages from tabulation machines were told to press a button that resulted in their votes not being counted.

Also in Arizona, the attorney general announced that mail-in ballots had been stolen from mailboxes and hidden under a rock.

President Donald Trump: (37:37)

In Clark County, Nevada, where most of the state's voters reside, the standards for matching a signature using the signature verification machine were intentionally lowered to allow large numbers of ballots to be counted that otherwise would never have passed muster. This machine was set at the lowest level. According to one report, in order to test the process, nine voters in Clark County cast ballots with intentionally incorrect signatures, and eight of the nine ballots were accepted and counted.

They said you could sign your name as Santa Claus, and it would be accepted.

Last week, the Clark County Commission threw out the results of a local election after the registrar reported finding, quote, "discrepancies that we can't explain."

Also in Nevada, some voters were entered into a raffle for more than a dozen gift cards worth as much as $250 if they could prove they had voted.

President Donald Trump: (38:42)
This took place on Indian reservations.

One of the most significant indications of widespread fraud is the extraordinarily low rejection rates for mail-in ballots in many key states.

These are the states that I had to win. In swing state after swing state, the number of ballots rejected has been dramatically lower than what would have been expected based on prior experience.

That means years and years of voting. In Georgia, just 0.2%, that's substantially less than 1%, of mail-in ballots have been rejected. In other words, almost none have been rejected. They took everything. Nothing was rejected, practically, compared to 6.4% in 2016. There are those that think that 6.4 was a low number.

President Donald Trump: (39:36)

Think of it. Almost none were rejected. The previous election, 6.4% were rejected.

We have seen similar declines in Pennsylvania, Nevada, and Michigan. Ballots weren't rejected, especially if they happen to be in Democrat areas. These irregularities are inexplicable unless there is a deliberate effort to accept ineligible ballots or fraudulent ballots.

President Donald Trump: (40:06)

In Pennsylvania, the secretary of state and the state supreme court in essence abolished signature verification requirements just weeks prior to the election, in violation of state law.

You're not allowed to do that. It has to be approved by the legislature. A judge can't do it. A state can't do it. An official can't do it. The only one that can do it is the legislature.

President Donald Trump: (40:33)

The reason for this is clear. They were not verifying signatures because they know the ballots have not been filled out by the voters in whose names they were cast.

In other words, people filled them out that had nothing to do with the names on the ballot.

A simple recount of the ballots under these circumstances only compounds the fraud. The only way to determine whether there was an honest vote is to conduct a full review of the envelopes in the relevant states. You will find that many of them, tens of thousands, have fraudulent signatures.

A full forensic audit is required to ensure that only legal ballots from lawfully registered voters that were properly cast are included in the final count.

President Donald Trump: (41:25)

This election is about great voter fraud, fraud that has never been seen like this before. It's about poll watchers who were not allowed to watch.

So illegal. It's about ballots that poured
in, and nobody but a few knew where
they came from. They were counted, and
they weren't for me. It's about big leads
on election night, tremendous leads,
leads where I was being congratulated
for a decisive easy victory.

All of a sudden, by morning or a couple
of days later, those leads rapidly
evaporated. It's about numbers of ballots
that were sent that nobody know where
they came from.

It's about machinery that was defective,
machinery that was stopped during
certain parts of the evening, miraculously
to open with more votes.

President Donald Trump: (42:24)

It was about many other things, but above all, it was about fraud. This election was rigged. Everybody knows it. I don't mind if I lose an election, but I want to lose an election fair and square.

What I don't want to do is have it stolen from the American people.

That's what we're fighting for. We have no choice to be doing that. We already have the proof.

We already have the evidence, and it's very clear. Many people in the media and even judges so far have refused to accept it.

They know it's true. They know it's there. They know who won the election,

but they refuse to say, "You're right."
Our country needs somebody to say,
"You're right."

President Donald Trump: (43:12)

Ultimately, I am prepared to accept any
accurate election result, and I hope that
Joe Biden is as well. We already have the
proof.

We already have tens of thousands of
ballots more than we need to overturn all
of these states that we're talking about.
This is an election for the highest office
in the greatest country in the history of
the world.

Every reasonable American should be
able to agree, based on what we have
already documented, that we need a

systematic analysis of the mail-in ballots to review the envelopes.

It's about the signature. If they're on the envelopes, we can only review the envelopes, and that will tell us everything.

President Donald Trump: (44:01)

This is the absolute minimum we should expect.

This is not just about my campaign, although it has a lot to do with who's going to be your next president.

This is about restoring faith and confidence in American elections.

This is about our democracy and the sacred rights that generations of Americans have fought, bled, and died to secure.

Nothing is more urgent or more important.

The only ballots that should count in this election are those cast by eligible voters who are citizens of our country, residents of the states in which they voted, and who cast their ballots in a lawful manner before the legal deadline.

President Donald Trump: (44:43)

Moreover, we must never again have an election in which there is not a reliable and transparent system to verify the eligibility, identity, and residency of every single person who casts a ballot, a very, very cherished ballot.

Many very smart people have congratulated me on all we've done: the biggest tax cuts in history, regulation cuts, the biggest in history.

We rebuilt our military. We took care of our vets like never before, Space Force, and so much more. Then they went on to say, as big and as important as these events were, the single greatest achievement in your presidency will be exactly what you're doing right now: voter integrity for our nation. It's more important than any of the things that we discussed.

President Donald Trump: (45:40)

If we don't root out the fraud, the tremendous and horrible fraud that's taken place in our 2020 election, we don't have a country anymore.

With the resolve and support of the American people, we will restore honesty and integrity to our elections.

We will restore trust in our system of government.

Thank you. God bless you. God bless America.

# Biden's Speech the Soul of a Nation

THE PRESIDENT:  My fellow Americans, please, if you have a seat, take it.  I speak to you tonight from sacred ground in America: Independence Hall in Philadelphia, Pennsylvania.

This is where America made its Declaration of Independence to the world more than two centuries ago with an idea, unique among nations, that in America, we're all created equal.

This is where the United States Constitution was written and debated.

This is where we set in motion the most extraordinary experiment of self-government the world has ever known with three simple words: "We, the People." "We, the People."

These two documents and the ideas they embody — equality and democracy — are the rock upon which this nation is built. They are how we became the greatest nation on Earth. They are why, for more than two centuries, America has been a beacon to the world.

But as I stand here tonight, equality and democracy are under assault. We do ourselves no favor to pretend otherwise.

So tonight, I have come this place where it all began to speak as plainly as I can to the nation about the threats we face, about the power we have in our own hands to meet these threats, and about the incredible future that lies in front of us if only we choose it.

We must never forget: We, the people, are the true heirs of the American experiment that began more than two centuries ago.

We, the people, have burning inside each of us the flame of liberty that was lit here at Independence Hall — a flame that lit our way through abolition, the Civil War, Suffrage, the Great Depression, world wars, Civil Rights.

That sacred flame still burns now in our time as we build an America that is more prosperous, free, and just.

That is the work of my presidency, a mission I believe in with my whole soul.

But first, we must be honest with each other and with ourselves.

Too much of what's happening in our country today is not normal.

Donald Trump and the MAGA Republicans represent an extremism that threatens the very foundations of our republic.

Now, I want to be very clear — (applause) — very clear up front: Not every Republican, not even the majority of Republicans, are MAGA Republicans. Not every Republican embraces their extreme ideology.

I know because I've been able to work with these mainstream Republicans.

But there is no question that the Republican Party today is dominated, driven, and intimidated by Donald Trump and the MAGA Republicans, and that is a threat to this country.

These are hard things.

But I'm an American President — not the President of red America or blue America, but of all America.

And I believe it is my duty — my duty to level with you, to tell the truth no matter how difficult, no matter how painful.

And here, in my view, is what is true: MAGA Republicans do not respect the Constitution. They do not believe in the rule of law. They do not recognize the will of the people.

They refuse to accept the results of a free election. And they're working right now, as I speak, in state after state to give power to decide elections in America to partisans and cronies, empowering election deniers to undermine democracy itself.

MAGA forces are determined to take this country backwards — backwards to an America where there is no right to choose, no right to privacy, no right to contraception, no right to marry who you love.

They promote authoritarian leaders, and they fan the flames of political violence that are a threat to our personal rights, to the pursuit of justice, to the rule of law, to the very soul of this country.

They look at the mob that stormed the United States Capitol on January 6th — brutally attacking law enforcement — not as insurrectionists who placed a dagger to the throat of our democracy, but they look at them as patriots.

And they see their MAGA failure to stop a peaceful transfer of power after the 2020 election as preparation for the 2022 and 2024 elections.

They tried everything last time to nullify the votes of 81 million people.  This time, they're determined to succeed in thwarting the will of the people.

That's why respected conservatives, like Federal Circuit Court Judge Michael Luttig, has called Trump and the extreme MAGA Republicans, quote, a "clear and present danger" to our democracy.

But while the threat to American democracy is real, I want to say as clearly as we can: We are not powerless in the face of these threats. We are not bystanders in this ongoing attack on democracy.

There are far more Americans — far more Americans from every — from every background and belief who reject

the extreme MAGA ideology than those
that accept it.  (Applause.)

And, folks, it is within our power, it's in
our hands — yours and mine — to stop
the assault on American democracy.

I believe America is at an inflection point
— one of those moments that determine
the shape of everything that's to come
after.

And now America must choose: to move
forward or to move backwards?  To
build the future or obsess about the
past?  To be a nation of hope and unity
and optimism, or a nation of fear,
division, and of darkness?

MAGA Republicans have made their choice. They embrace anger. They thrive on chaos. They live not in the light of truth but in the shadow of lies.

But together — together, we can choose a different path. We can choose a better path. Forward, to the future. A future of possibility. A future to build and dream and hope.

And we're on that path, moving ahead.

I know this nation. I know you, the American people. I know your courage. I know your hearts. And I know our history.

This is a nation that honors our Constitution.  We do not reject it.  (Applause.)

This is a nation that believes in the rule of law.  We do not repudiate it.  (Applause.)

This is a nation that respects free and fair elections.  We honor the will of the people.  We do not deny it.  (Applause.)

And this is a nation that rejects violence as a political tool.  We do not encourage violence.

We are still an America that believes in honesty and decency and respect for others, patriotism, liberty, justice for all, hope, possibilities.

We are still, at our core, a democracy.
(Applause.)

And yet history tells us that blind loyalty
to a single leader and a willingness to
engage in political violence is fatal to
democracy.

For a long time, we've told ourselves that
American democracy is guaranteed, but
it's not.

We have to defend it, protect it, stand up
for it — each and every one of us.

That's why tonight I'm asking our nation
to come together, unite behind the single

purpose of defending our democracy
regardless of your ideology.  (Applause.)

We're all called, by duty and conscience,
to confront extremists who will put their
own pursuit of power above all else.

Democrats, independents, mainstream
Republicans: We must be stronger, more
determined, and more committed to
saving American democracy than
MAGA Republicans are to — to
destroying American democracy.

We, the people, will not let anyone or
anything tear us apart.  Today, there are
dangers around us we cannot allow to
prevail.  We hear — you've heard it —
more and more talk about violence as an
acceptable political tool in this country.

It's not.  It can never be an acceptable tool.

So I want to say this plain and simple: There is no place for political violence in America.  Period.  None.  Ever. (Applause.)

We saw law enforcement brutally attacked on January the 6th.  We've seen election officials, poll workers — many of them volunteers of both parties — subjected to intimidation and death threats.  And — can you believe it? — FBI agents just doing their job as directed, facing threats to their own lives from their own fellow citizens.

On top of that, there are public figures — today, yesterday, and the day before

— predicting and all but calling for mass violence and rioting in the streets.

This is inflammatory.  It's dangerous.  It's against the rule of law.  And we, the people, must say: This is not who we are.  (Applause.)

Ladies and gentlemen, we can't be pro-ex- — pro-ex- — pro-insurrectionist and pro-American.  They're incompatible.  (Applause.)

We can't allow violence to be normalized in this country.  It's wrong.  We each have to reject political violence with — with all the moral clarity and conviction this nation can muster.  Now.

We can't let the integrity of our elections
be undermined, for that is a path to
chaos.

Look, I know poli- — politics can be
fierce and mean and nasty in America.  I
get it.  I believe in the give-and-take of
politics, in disagreement and debate and
dissent.

We're a big, complicated country.  But
democracy endures only if we, the
people, respect the guardrails of the
republic.  Only if we, the people, accept
the results of free and fair elections.
(Applause.)  Only if we, the people, see
politics not as total war but mediation of
our differences.

Democracy cannot survive when one side believes there are only two outcomes to an election: either they win or they were cheated.  And that's where MAGA Republicans are today. (Applause.)

They don't understand what every patriotic American knows: You can't love your country only when you win. (Applause.)  It's fundamental.

American democracy only works only if we choose to respect the rule of law and the institutions that were set up in this chamber behind me, only if we respect our legitimate political differences.

I will not stand by and watch — I will not — the will of the American people

be overturned by wild conspiracy
theories and baseless, evidence-free
claims of fraud.

I will not stand by and watch elections in
this country stolen by people who simply
refuse to accept that they lost.
(Applause.)

I will not stand by and watch the most
fundamental freedom in this country —
the freedom to vote and have your vote
counted — and — be taken from you
and the American people.  (Applause.)

Look, as your President, I will defend
our democracy with every fiber of my
being, and I'm asking every American to
join me.  (Applause.)

(A protestor disruption can be heard.)

Throughout our history, America has often made the greatest progress coming out of some of our darkest moments, like you're hearing in that bullhorn.

I believe we can and we must do that again, and we are.

MAGA Republicans look at America and see carnage and darkness and despair. They spread fear and lies –- lies told for profit and power.

But I see a very different America — an America with an unlimited future, an America that is about to take off.  I hope you see it as well.  Just look around.

I believed we could lift America from the depths of COVID, so we passed the largest economic recovery package since Franklin Delano Roosevelt.  And today, America's economy is faster, stronger than any other advanced nation in the world.  (Applause.)  We have more to go.

I believed we could build a better America, so we passed the biggest infrastructure investment since President Dwight D. Eisenhower.  And we've now embarked on a decade of rebuilding

the nation's roads, bridges, highways, ports, water systems, high-speed Internet, railroads.  (Applause.)

I believed we could make America safer, so we passed the most significant gun safety law since President Clinton. (Applause.)

I believed we could go from being the highest cost of prescriptions in the world to making prescription drugs and healthcare more affordable, so we passed the most significant healthcare reforms since President Obama signed the Affordable Care Act.  (Applause.)

And I believed we could create — we could create a clean energy future and save the planet, so we passed the most important climate initiative ever, ever, ever.  (Applause.)

The cynics and the critics tell us nothing can get done, but they are wrong.  There is not a single thing America cannot do

— not a single thing beyond our capacity if we do it together.

It's never easy. But we're proving that in America, no matter how long the road, progress does come. (Applause.)

Look, I know the last year — few years have been tough. But today, COVID no longer controls our lives. More Americans are working than ever. Businesses are growing. Our schools are open. Millions of Americans have been lifted out of poverty. Millions of veterans once exposed to toxic burn pits will now get what they deserve for their families and the compa- — compensation. (Applause.)

American manufacturing has come alive across the Heartland, and the future will be made in America — (applause) — no matter what the white supremacists and the extremists say.

I made a bet on you, the American people, and that bet is paying off. Proving that from darkness — the darkness of Charlottesville, of COVID, of gun violence, of insurrection — we can see the light.  Light is now visible. (Applause.)

Light that will guide us forward not only in words, but in actions — actions for you, for your children, for your grandchildren, for America.

Even in this moment, with all the challenges we face, I give you my word as a Biden: I've never been more optimistic about America's future.  Not because of me, but because of who you are.

We're going to end cancer as we know it. Mark my words.  (Applause.)

We are going to create millions of new jobs in a clean energy economy.

We're going to think big.  We're going to make the 21st century another American century because the world needs us to. (Applause.)

That's where we need to focus our energy — not in the past, not on divisive culture wars, not on the politics of grievance, but on a future we can build together.

The MAGA Republicans believe that for them to succeed, everyone else has to fail. They believe America — not like I believe about America.

I believe America is big enough for all of us to succeed, and that is the nation we're building: a nation where no one is left behind.

I ran for President because I believed we were in a battle for the soul of this nation. I still believe that to be true. I believe the soul is the breath, the life, and the essence of who we are. The soul is what makes us "us."

The soul of America is defined by the sacred proposition that all are created equal in the image of God.  That all are entitled to be treated with decency, dignity, and respect.  That all deserve justice and a shot at lives of prosperity and consequence.  And that democracy — democracy must be defended, for democracy makes all these things possible.  (Applause.)  Folks, and it's up to us.

Democracy begins and will be preserved in we, the people's, habits of heart, in our character: optimism that is tested

yet endures, courage that digs deep when we need it, empathy that fuels democracy, the willingness to see each other not as enemies but as fellow Americans.

Look, our democracy is imperfect.  It
always has been.

Notwithstanding those folks you hear on
the other side there.  They're entitled to
be outrageous.  This is a democracy.  But
history and common sense — (applause)
— good manners is nothing they've ever
suffered from.

But history and common sense tell us
that opportunity, liberty, and justice for
all are most likely to come to pass in a
democracy.

We have never fully realized the
aspirations of our founding, but every
generation has opened those doors a

little wider to include more people who have been excluded before.

My fellow Americans, America is an idea — the most powerful idea in the history of the world.  And it beats in the hearts of the people of this country.  It beats in all of our hearts.  It unites America.  It is the American creed.

The idea that America guarantees that everyone be treated with dignity.  It gives hate no safe harbor.  It installs in everyone the belief that no matter where you start in life, there's nothing you can't achieve.

That's who we are.  That's what we stand for.  That's what we believe.  And that is precisely what we are doing: opening doors, creating new possibilities, focusing on the future.  And we're only just beginning.  (Applause.)

Our task is to make our nation free and fair, just and strong, noble and whole.

And this work is the work of democracy — the work of this generation.  It is the work of our time, for all time.

We can't afford to have — leave anyone on the sidelines.  We need everyone to do their part.  So speak up.  Speak out. Get engaged.  Vote, vote, vote. (Applause.)

And if we all do our duty — if we do our duty in 2022 and beyond, then ages still to come will say we — all of us here —

we kept the faith. We preserved democracy. (Applause.) We heeded our wor- — we — we heeded not our worst instincts but our better angels. And we proved that, for all its imperfections, America is still the beacon to the world, an ideal to be realized, a promise to be kept.

There is nothing more important, nothing more sacred, nothing more American. That's our soul. That's who we truly are. And that's who must — we must always be.

And I have no doubt — none — that this is who we will be and that we'll come together as a nation. That we'll secure our democracy. That for the next 200 years, we'll have what we had the past 200 years: the greatest nation on the face of the Earth.

We just need to remember who we are. We are the United States of America. The United States of America. (Applause.)

And may God protect our nation. And may God protect all those who stand watch over our democracy. God bless you all. (Applause.) Democracy. Thank you. (Applause.)

https://www.youtube.com/watch?v=JemWkV2Vcic

# State of the Union Address

Mr. Speaker. Madam Vice President. Our First Lady and Second Gentleman.

Members of Congress and the Cabinet. Leaders of our military.

Mr. Chief Justice, Associate Justices, and retired Justices of the Supreme Court.

And you, my fellow Americans.

I start tonight by congratulating the members of the 118th Congress and the new Speaker of the House, Kevin McCarthy.

Mr. Speaker, I look forward to working together.

I also want to congratulate the new leader of the House Democrats and the first Black House Minority Leader in history, Hakeem Jeffries.

Congratulations to the longest serving Senate Leader in history, Mitch McConnell.

And congratulations to Chuck Schumer for another term as Senate Majority Leader, this time with an even bigger majority.

And I want to give special recognition to someone who I think will be considered the greatest Speaker in the history of this country, Nancy Pelosi.

The story of America is a story of progress and resilience. Of always moving forward. Of never giving up.

A story that is unique among all nations.

We are the only country that has emerged from every crisis stronger than when we entered it.

That is what we are doing again.

Two years ago, our economy was reeling.

As I stand here tonight, we have created a record 12 million new jobs, more jobs created in two years than any president has ever created in four years.

Two years ago, COVID had shut down our businesses, closed our schools, and robbed us of so much.

Today, COVID no longer controls our lives.

And two years ago, our democracy faced its greatest threat since the Civil War.

Today, though bruised, our democracy remains unbowed and unbroken.

As we gather here tonight, we are writing the next chapter in the great American story, a story of progress and resilience. When world leaders ask me to define America, I define our country in one word: Possibilities.

You know, we're often told that Democrats and Republicans can't work together.

But over these past two years, we proved the cynics and the naysayers wrong.

Yes, we disagreed plenty. And yes, there were times when Democrats had to go it alone.

But time and again, Democrats and Republicans came together.

Came together to defend a stronger and safer Europe.

Came together to pass a once-in-a-generation infrastructure law, building bridges to connect our nation and people.

Came together to pass one of the most significant laws ever, helping veterans exposed to toxic burn pits.

In fact, I signed over 300 bipartisan laws since becoming President. From reauthorizing the Violence Against Women Act, to the Electoral Count Reform Act, to the Respect for Marriage Act that protects the right to marry the person you love.

To my Republican friends, if we could work together in the last Congress, there is no reason we can't work together in this new Congress.

The people sent us a clear message. Fighting for the sake of fighting, power for the sake of power, conflict for the sake of conflict, gets us nowhere.

And that's always been my vision for our country.

To restore the soul of the nation.

To rebuild the backbone of America, the middle class.

To unite the country.

We've been sent here to finish the job.

For decades, the middle class was hollowed out.

Too many good-paying manufacturing jobs moved overseas. Factories at home closed down.

Once-thriving cities and towns became shadows of what they used to be.

And along the way, something else was lost.

Pride. That sense of self-worth.

I ran for President to fundamentally change things, to make sure the economy works for everyone so we can all feel pride in what we do.

To build an economy from the bottom up and the middle out, not from the top down. Because when the middle class does well, the poor have a ladder up and the wealthy still do very well. We all do well.

As my Dad used to say, a job is about a lot more than a paycheck. It's about your dignity. It's about respect. It's about being able to look your kid in the eye and say, "Honey —it's going to be OK," and mean it.

So, let's look at the results.
Unemployment rate at 3.4%, a 50-year
low. Near record low unemployment for
Black and Hispanic workers.

We've already created 800,000 good-
paying manufacturing jobs, the fastest
growth in 40 years.

Where is it written that America can't
lead the world in manufacturing again?

For too many decades, we imported
products and exported jobs.

Now, thanks to all we've done, we're
exporting American products and
creating American jobs.

Inflation has been a global problem because of the pandemic that disrupted supply chains and Putin's war that disrupted energy and food supplies.

But we're better positioned than any country on Earth.

We have more to do, but here at home, inflation is coming down.

Here at home, gas prices are down $1.50 a gallon since their peak.

Food inflation is coming down.

Inflation has fallen every month for the last six months while take home pay has gone up.

Additionally, over the last two years, a record 10 million Americans applied to start a new small business.

Every time somebody starts a small business, it's an act of hope.

And the Vice President will continue her work to ensure more small businesses can access capital and the historic laws we enacted.

Standing here last year, I shared with you a story of American genius and possibility.

Semiconductors, the small computer chips the size of your fingertip that power everything from cellphones to automobiles, and so much more. These chips were invented right here in America.

America used to make nearly 40% of the world's chips.

But in the last few decades, we lost our edge and we're down to producing only 10%. We all saw what happened during the pandemic when chip factories overseas shut down.

Today's automobiles need up to 3,000 chips each, but American automakers couldn't make enough cars because there weren't enough chips.

Car prices went up. So did everything from refrigerators to cellphones.

We can never let that happen again.

That's why we came together to pass the bipartisan CHIPS and Science Act.

We're making sure the supply chain for America begins in America.

We've already created 800,000 manufacturing jobs even without this law.

With this new law, we will create hundreds of thousands of new jobs across the country.

That's going to come from companies that have announced more than $300 billion in investments in American manufacturing in the last two years.

Outside of Columbus, Ohio, Intel is building semiconductor factories on a thousand acres – a literal field of dreams.

That'll create 10,000 jobs. 7,000 construction jobs. 3,000 jobs once the factories are finished.

Jobs paying $130,000 a year, and many don't require a college degree.

Jobs where people don't have to leave home in search of opportunity.

And it's just getting started.

Think about the new homes, new small businesses, and so much more that will come to life.

Talk to mayors and Governors, Democrats and Republicans, and they'll tell you what this means to their communities.

We're seeing these fields of dreams transform the heartland.

But to maintain the strongest economy in the world, we also need the best infrastructure in the world.

We used to be #1 in the world in infrastructure, then we fell to #13th.

Now we're coming back because we came together to pass the Bipartisan Infrastructure Law, the largest investment in infrastructure since President Eisenhower's Interstate Highway System.

Already, we've funded over 20,000 projects, including at major airports from Boston to Atlanta to Portland.

These projects will put hundreds of thousands of people to work rebuilding our highways, bridges, railroads, tunnels, ports and airports, clean water, and high-speed internet across America.

Urban. Suburban. Rural. Tribal.

And we're just getting started. I sincerely thank my Republican friends who voted for the law.

And to my Republican friends who voted against it but still ask to fund projects in their districts, don't worry.

I promised to be the president for all Americans.

We'll fund your projects. And I'll see you at the ground-breaking.

This law will help further unite all of America.

Major projects like the Brent Spence bridge between Kentucky and Ohio over the Ohio River. Built 60 years ago. Badly in need of repairs.

One of the nation's most congested freight routes carrying $2 billion worth of freight every day. Folks have been talking about fixing it for decades, but we're finally going to get it done.

I went there last month with Democrats and Republicans from both states to deliver $1.6 billion for this project.

While I was there, I met an ironworker named Sara, who is here tonight.

For 30 years, she's been a proud member of Ironworkers Local 44, known as the "cowboys of the sky" who built the Cincinnati skyline.

Sara said she can't wait to be ten stories above the Ohio River building that new bridge. That's pride.

That's what we're also building – Pride.

We're also replacing poisonous lead pipes that go into 10 million homes and 400,000 schools and childcare centers, so every child in America can drink clean water.

We're making sure that every community has access to affordable, high-speed internet.

No parent should have to drive to a McDonald's parking lot so their kid can do their homework online.

And when we do these projects, we're going to Buy American.

Buy American has been the law of the land since 1933. But for too long, past administrations have found ways to get around it.

Not anymore.

Tonight, I'm also announcing new standards to require all construction materials used in federal infrastructure projects to be made in America.

American-made lumber, glass, drywall, fiber optic cables.

And on my watch, American roads, American bridges, and American highways will be made with American products.

My economic plan is about investing in places and people that have been forgotten. Amid the economic upheaval of the past four decades, too many people have been left behind or treated like they're invisible.

Maybe that's you, watching at home.

You remember the jobs that went away. And you wonder whether a path even exists anymore for you and your children to get ahead without moving away.

I get it.

That's why we're building an economy where no one is left behind.

Jobs are coming back, pride is coming back, because of the choices we made in the last two years. This is a blue-collar blueprint to rebuild America and make a real difference in your lives.

For example, too many of you lay in bed at night staring at the ceiling, wondering what will happen if your spouse gets cancer, your child gets sick, or if something happens to you.

Will you have the money to pay your medical bills? Will you have to sell the house?

I get it. With the Inflation Reduction Act that I signed into law, we're taking on powerful interests to bring your health care costs down so you can sleep better at night.

You know, we pay more for prescription drugs than any major country on Earth.

For example, one in ten Americans has diabetes.

Every day, millions need insulin to control their diabetes so they can stay

alive. Insulin has been around for 100
years. It costs drug companies just $10 a
vial to make.

But, Big Pharma has been unfairly
charging people hundreds of dollars –
and making record profits.

Not anymore.

We capped the cost of insulin at $35 a
month for seniors on Medicare.

But there are millions of other
Americans who are not on Medicare,
including 200,000 young people with
Type I diabetes who need insulin to save
their lives.

Let's finish the job this time.

Let's cap the cost of insulin at $35 a month for every American who needs it.

This law also caps out-of-pocket drug costs for seniors on Medicare at a maximum $2,000 per year when there are in fact many drugs, like expensive cancer drugs, that can cost up to $10,000, $12,000, and $14,000 a year.

If drug prices rise faster than inflation, drug companies will have to pay Medicare back the difference.

And we're finally giving Medicare the power to negotiate drug prices. Bringing down prescription drug costs doesn't just save seniors money.

It will cut the federal deficit, saving tax payers hundreds of billions of dollars on the prescription drugs the government buys for Medicare.

Why wouldn't we want to do that?

Now, some members here are threatening to repeal the Inflation Reduction Act.

Make no mistake, if you try to do anything to raise the cost of prescription drugs, I will veto it.

I'm pleased to say that more Americans have health insurance now than ever in history.

A record 16 million people are enrolled under the Affordable Care Act.

Thanks to the law I signed last year, millions are saving $800 a year on their premiums.

But the way that law was written, that benefit expires after 2025.

Let's finish the job, make those savings permanent, and expand coverage to those left off Medicaid.

Look, the Inflation Reduction Act is also the most significant investment ever to tackle the climate crisis.

Lowering utility bills, creating American jobs, and leading the world to a clean energy future.

I've visited the devastating aftermaths of record floods and droughts, storms and wildfires.

In addition to emergency recovery from Puerto Rico to Florida to Idaho, we are rebuilding for the long term.

New electric grids able to weather the next major storm.

Roads and water systems to withstand the next big flood.

Clean energy to cut pollution and create jobs in communities too often left behind.

We're building 500,000 electric vehicle charging stations installed across the country by tens of thousands of IBEW workers.

And helping families save more than $1,000 a year with tax credits for the purchase of electric vehicles and energy-efficient appliances.

Historic conservation efforts to be responsible stewards of our lands.

Let's face reality.

The climate crisis doesn't care if your state is red or blue. It is an existential threat.

We have an obligation to our children and grandchildren to confront it. I'm proud of how America is at last stepping up to the challenge.

But there's so much more to do.

We will finish the job.

And we pay for these investments in our future by finally making the wealthiest and the biggest corporations begin to pay their fair share.

I'm a capitalist. But just pay your fair share.

And I think a lot of you at home agree with me that our present tax system is simply unfair.

The idea that in 2020, 55 of the biggest companies in America made $40 billion in profits and paid zero in federal income taxes?

That's simply not fair.

But now, because of the law I signed, billion-dollar companies have to pay a minimum of 15%.

Just 15%.

That's less than a nurse pays. Let me be clear.

Under my plan, nobody earning less than $400,000 a year will pay an additional penny in taxes.

Nobody. Not one penny.

But there's more to do.

Let's finish the job. Reward work, not just wealth. Pass my proposal for a billionaire minimum tax.

Because no billionaire should pay a lower tax rate than a school teacher or a firefighter.

You may have noticed that Big Oil just reported record profits.

Last year, they made $200 billion in the midst of a global energy crisis.

It's outrageous.

They invested too little of that profit to increase domestic production and keep gas prices down.

Instead, they used those record profits to buy back their own stock, rewarding their CEOs and shareholders.

Corporations ought to do the right thing.

That's why I propose that we quadruple the tax on corporate stock buybacks to encourage long term investments instead.

They will still make a considerable profit.

Let's finish the job and close the loopholes that allow the very wealthy to avoid paying their taxes.

Instead of cutting the number of audits of wealthy tax payers, I signed a law that will reduce the deficit by $114 billion by cracking down on wealthy tax cheats.

That's being fiscally responsible.

In the last two years, my administration cut the deficit by more than $1.7 trillion – the largest deficit reduction in American history.

Under the previous administration, America's deficit went up four years in a row.

Because of those record deficits, no president added more to the national debt in any four years than my predecessor.

Nearly 25% of the entire national debt, a debt that took 200 years to accumulate, was added by that administration alone.

How did Congress respond to all that debt?

They lifted the debt ceiling three times without preconditions or crisis.

They paid America's bills to prevent economic disaster for our country.

Tonight, I'm asking this Congress to follow suit.

Let us commit here tonight that the full faith and credit of the United States of America will never, ever be questioned.

Some of my Republican friends want to take the economy hostage unless I agree to their economic plans. All of you at home should know what their plans are.

Instead of making the wealthy pay their fair share, some Republicans want Medicare and Social Security to sunset every five years.

That means if Congress doesn't vote to keep them, those programs will go away.

Other Republicans say if we don't cut Social Security and Medicare, they'll let America default on its debt for the first time in our history.

I won't let that happen.

Social Security and Medicare are a lifeline for millions of seniors.

Americans have been paying into them with every single paycheck since they started working.

So tonight, let's all agree to stand up for seniors. Stand up and show them we will not cut Social Security. We will not cut Medicare.

Those benefits belong to the American people. They earned them.

If anyone tries to cut Social Security, I will stop them. And if anyone tries to cut Medicare, I will stop them.

I will not allow them to be taken away.

Not today. Not tomorrow. Not ever.

Next month when I offer my fiscal plan, I ask my Republican friends to offer their plan.

We can sit down together and discuss both plans together.

My plan will lower the deficit by $2 trillion.

I won't cut a single Social Security or Medicare benefit.

In fact, I will extend the Medicare Trust Fund by at least two decades.

I will not raise taxes on anyone making under $400,000 a year. And I will pay for the ideas I've talked about tonight by making the wealthy and big corporations begin to pay their fair share.

Look, here's the deal. Big corporations aren't just taking advantage of the tax code. They're taking advantage of you, the American consumer.

Here's my message to all of you out there: I have your back. We're already preventing insurance companies from sending surprise medical bills, stopping 1 million surprise bills a month.

We're protecting seniors' lives and life savings by cracking down on nursing homes that commit fraud, endanger patient safety, or prescribe drugs they don't need.

Millions of Americans can now save thousands of dollars because they can finally get hearing aids over-the-counter without a prescription.

Capitalism without competition is not capitalism. It is exploitation.

Last year I cracked down on foreign shipping companies that were making you pay higher prices for everyday goods coming into our country.

I signed a bipartisan bill that cut shipping costs by 90%, helping American farmers, businesses, and consumers.

Let's finish the job.

Pass bipartisan legislation to strengthen antitrust enforcement and prevent big online platforms from giving their own products an unfair advantage.

My administration is also taking on "junk" fees, those hidden surcharges too many businesses use to make you pay more.

For example, we're making airlines show you the full ticket price upfront and refund your money if your flight is cancelled or delayed.

We've reduced exorbitant bank overdraft fees, saving consumers more than $1 billion a year.

We're cutting credit card late fees by 75%, from $30 to $8.

Junk fees may not matter to the very wealthy, but they matter to most folks in homes like the one I grew up in. They add up to hundreds of dollars a month.

They make it harder for you to pay the bills or afford that family trip.

I know how unfair it feels when a company overcharges you and gets away with it.

Not anymore.

We've written a bill to stop all that. It's called the Junk Fee Prevention Act.

We'll ban surprise "resort fees" that hotels tack on to your bill. These fees can cost you up to $90 a night at hotels that aren't even resorts.

We'll make cable internet and cellphone companies stop charging you up to $200 or more when you decide to switch to another provider.

We'll cap service fees on tickets to concerts and sporting events and make companies disclose all fees upfront.

And we'll prohibit airlines from charging up to $50 roundtrip for families just to sit together.

Baggage fees are bad enough – they can't just treat your child like a piece of luggage.

Americans are tired of being played for suckers.

Pass the Junk Fee Prevention Act so companies stop ripping us off.

For too long, workers have been getting stiffed.

Not anymore.

We're beginning to restore the dignity of work.

For example, 30 million workers had to sign non-compete agreements when they took a job. So a cashier at a burger place can't cross the street to take the same job at another burger place to make a couple bucks more.

Not anymore.

We're banning those agreements so companies have to compete for workers and pay them what they're worth.

I'm so sick and tired of companies breaking the law by preventing workers from organizing.

Pass the PRO Act because workers have a right to form a union. And let's guarantee all workers a living wage.

Let's also make sure working parents can afford to raise a family with sick days, paid family and medical leave, and affordable child care that will enable millions more people to go to work.

Let's also restore the full Child Tax Credit, which gave tens of millions of parents some breathing room and cut child poverty in half, to the lowest level in history.

And by the way, when we do all of these things, we increase productivity. We increase economic growth.

Let's also finish the job and get more families access to affordable and quality housing.

Let's get seniors who want to stay in
their homes the care they need to do so.
And give a little more breathing room to
millions of family caregivers looking
after their loved ones.

Pass my plan so we get seniors and
people with disabilities the home care
services they need and support the
workers who are doing God's work.

These plans are fully paid for and we can
afford to do them.

Restoring the dignity of work also means
making education an affordable ticket to
the middle class.

When we made 12 years of public education universal in the last century, it made us the best-educated, best-prepared nation in the world.

But the world has caught up.

Jill, who teaches full-time, has an expression: "Any nation that out-educates us will out-compete us."

Folks, you all know 12 years is not enough to win the economic competition for the 21st Century.

If you want America to have the best-educated workforce, let's finish the job by providing access to pre-school for 3- and 4-year-olds.

Studies show that children who go to pre-school are nearly 50% more likely to finish high school and go on to earn a 2- or 4-year degree, no matter their background.

Let's give public school teachers a raise.

And we're making progress by reducing student debt and increasing Pell Grants for working- and middle-class families.

Let's finish the job, connect students to career opportunities starting in high school and provide two years of community college, some of the best career training in America, in addition to being a pathway to a four-year degree.

Let's offer every American the path to a good career whether they go to college or not.

And folks, in the midst of the COVID crisis when schools were closed, let's also recognize how far we've come in the fight against the pandemic itself.

While the virus is not gone, thanks to the resilience of the American people, we have broken COVID's grip on us.

COVID deaths are down nearly 90%.

We've saved millions of lives and opened our country back up.

And soon we'll end the public health emergency.

But we will remember the toll and pain that will never go away for so many. More than 1 million Americans have lost their lives to COVID.

Families grieving. Children orphaned. Empty chairs at the dining room table.

We remember them, and we remain vigilant.

We still need to monitor dozens of variants and support new vaccines and treatments.

So Congress needs to fund these efforts and keep America safe.

And as we emerge from this crisis stronger, I'm also doubling down on prosecuting criminals who stole relief money meant to keep workers and small businesses afloat during the pandemic.

Before I came to office many inspector generals who protect taxpayer dollars were sidelined. Fraud was rampant.

Last year, I told you the watchdogs are back. Since then, we've recovered billions of taxpayer dollars.

Now, let's triple our anti-fraud strike forces going after these criminals, double the statute of limitations on these crimes, and crack down on identity fraud by criminal syndicates stealing billions of dollars from the American people.

For every dollar we put into fighting fraud, taxpayers get back at least ten times as much.

COVID left other scars, like the spike in violent crime in 2020, the first year of the pandemic.

We have an obligation to make sure all our people are safe.

Public safety depends on public trust. But too often that trust is violated.

Joining us tonight are the parents of Tyre Nichols, who had to bury him just last week. There are no words to describe the heartbreak and grief of losing a child.

But imagine what it's like to lose a child at the hands of the law.

Imagine having to worry whether your son or daughter will come home from walking down the street or playing in the park or just driving their car.

I've never had to have the talk with my children – Beau, Hunter, and Ashley – that so many Black and Brown families have had with their children.

If a police officer pulls you over, turn on your interior lights. Don't reach for your license. Keep your hands on the steering wheel.

Imagine having to worry like that every day in America.

Here's what Tyre's mom shared with me when I asked her how she finds the courage to carry on and speak out.

With faith in God, she said her son "was a beautiful soul and something good will come from this."

Imagine how much courage and character that takes.

It's up to us. It's up to all of us.

We all want the same thing.

Neighborhoods free of violence.

Law enforcement who earn the community's trust.

Our children to come home safely.

Equal protection under the law; that's the covenant we have with each other in America.

And we know police officers put their lives on the line every day, and we ask them to do too much.

To be counselors, social workers, psychologists; responding to drug overdoses, mental health crises, and more.

We ask too much of them.

I know most cops are good, decent people. They risk their lives every time they put on that shield.

But what happened to Tyre in Memphis happens too often.

We have to do better.

Give law enforcement the training they need, hold them to higher standards, and

help them succeed in keeping everyone
safe.

We also need more first responders and
other professionals to address growing
mental health and substance abuse
challenges.

More resources to reduce violent crime
and gun crime; more community
intervention programs; more
investments in housing, education, and
job training.

All this can help prevent violence in the
first place.

And when police officers or departments
violate the public's trust, we must hold
them accountable.

With the support of families of victims, civil rights groups, and law enforcement, I signed an executive order for all federal officers banning chokeholds, restricting no-knock warrants, and other key elements of the George Floyd Act.

Let's commit ourselves to make the words of Tyre's mother come true, something good must come from this.

All of us in this chamber, we need to rise to this moment.

We can't turn away.

Let's do what we know in our hearts we need to do.

Let's come together and finish the job on police reform.

Do something.

That was the same plea of parents who lost their children in Uvalde: Do something on gun violence.

Thank God we did, passing the most sweeping gun safety law in three decades.

That includes things that the majority of responsible gun owners support, like enhanced background checks for 18 to 21-year-olds and red flag laws keeping guns out of the hands of people who are a danger to themselves and others.

But we know our work is not done.

Joining us tonight is Brandon Tsay, a 26-year-old hero.

Brandon put off his college dreams to stay by his mom's side as she was dying from cancer. He now works at a dance studio started by his grandparents.

Two weeks ago, during Lunar New Year celebrations, he heard the studio's front door close and saw a man pointing a gun at him.

He thought he was going to die, but then he thought about the people inside.

In that instant, he found the courage to act and wrestled the semi-automatic pistol away from a gunman who had already killed 11 people at another dance studio.

He saved lives. It's time we do the same as well.

Ban assault weapons once and for all.

We did it before. I led the fight to ban them in 1994.

In the 10 years the ban was law, mass shootings went down. After Republicans let it expire, mass shootings tripled.

Let's finish the job and ban assault
weapons again.

And let's also come together on
immigration and make it a bipartisan
issue like it was before.

We now have a record number of
personnel working to secure the border,
arresting 8,000 human smugglers and
seizing over 23,000 pounds of fentanyl in
just the last several months.

Since we launched our new border plan
last month, unlawful migration from
Cuba, Haiti, Nicaragua, and Venezuela
has come down 97%.

But America's border problems won't be
fixed until Congress acts.

If you won't pass my comprehensive immigration reform, at least pass my plan to provide the equipment and officers to secure the border. And a pathway to citizenship for Dreamers, those on temporary status, farm workers, and essential workers.

Here in the people's House, it's our duty to protect all the people's rights and freedoms.

Congress must restore the right the Supreme Court took away last year and codify Roe v. Wade to protect every woman's constitutional right to choose.

The Vice President and I are doing everything we can to protect access to reproductive health care and safeguard patient privacy. But already, more than a dozen states are enforcing extreme abortion bans.

Make no mistake; if Congress passes a national abortion ban, I will veto it.

Let's also pass the bipartisan Equality Act to ensure LGBTQ Americans, especially transgender young people, can live with safety and dignity.

Our strength is not just the example of our power, but the power of our example. Let's remember the world is watching.

I spoke from this chamber one year ago, just days after Vladimir Putin unleashed his brutal war against Ukraine.

A murderous assault, evoking images of the death and destruction Europe suffered in World War II.

Putin's invasion has been a test for the ages. A test for America. A test for the world.

Would we stand for the most basic of principles?

Would we stand for sovereignty?

Would we stand for the right of people to live free from tyranny?

Would we stand for the defense of democracy?

For such a defense matters to us because it keeps the peace and prevents open season for would-be aggressors to threaten our security and prosperity. One year later, we know the answer.

Yes, we would.

And yes, we did.

Together, we did what America always does at our best.

We led.

We united NATO and built a global coalition.

We stood against Putin's aggression.

We stood with the Ukrainian people.

Tonight, we are once again joined by Ukraine's Ambassador to the United States. She represents not just her nation, but the courage of her people.

Ambassador, America is united in our support for your country. We will stand with you as long as it takes.

Our nation is working for more freedom, more dignity, and more peace, not just in Europe, but everywhere.

Before I came to office, the story was about how the People's Republic of

China was increasing its power and America was falling in the world.

Not anymore.

I've made clear with President Xi that we seek competition, not conflict.

I will make no apologies that we are investing to make America strong. Investing in American innovation, in industries that will define the future, and that China's government is intent on dominating.

Investing in our alliances and working with our allies to protect our advanced technologies so they're not used against us.

Modernizing our military to safeguard stability and deter aggression.

Today, we're in the strongest position in decades to compete with China or anyone else in the world.

I am committed to work with China where it can advance American interests and benefit the world.

But make no mistake: as we made clear last week, if China's threatens our sovereignty, we will act to protect our country. And we did.

And let's be clear: winning the competition with China should unite all of us. We face serious challenges across the world.

But in the past two years, democracies have become stronger, not weaker.

Autocracies have grown weaker, not stronger.

America is rallying the world again to meet those challenges, from climate and global health, to food insecurity, to terrorism and territorial aggression.

Allies are stepping up, spending more and doing more.

And bridges are forming between partners in the Pacific and those in the Atlantic. And those who bet against America are learning just how wrong they are.

It's never a good bet to bet against America.

When I came to office, most everyone assumed bipartisanship was impossible. But I never believed it.

That's why a year ago, I offered a Unity Agenda for the nation.

We've made real progress.

Together, we passed a law making it easier for doctors to prescribe effective treatments for opioid addiction.

Passed a gun safety law making historic investments in mental health.

Launched ARPA-H to drive
breakthroughs in the fight against cancer,
Alzheimer's, diabetes, and so much
more.

We passed the Heath Robinson PACT
Act, named for the late Iraq war veteran
whose story about exposure to toxic
burn pits I shared here last year.

But there is so much more to do. And
we can do it together.

Joining us tonight is a father named
Doug from Newton, New Hampshire.

He wrote Jill and me a letter about his
daughter Courtney. Contagious laugh.
Her sister's best friend.

He shared a story all too familiar to millions of Americans.

Courtney discovered pills in high school. It spiraled into addiction and eventually her death from a fentanyl overdose.

She was 20 years old.

Describing the last eight years without her, Doug said, "There is no worse pain."

Yet their family has turned pain into purpose, working to end stigma and change laws.

He told us he wants to "start the journey towards America's recovery."

Doug, we're with you.

Fentanyl is killing more than 70,000 Americans a year.

Let's launch a major surge to stop fentanyl production, sale, and trafficking, with more drug detection machines to inspect cargo and stop pills and powder at the border.

Working with couriers like Fed Ex to inspect more packages for drugs. Strong penalties to crack down on fentanyl trafficking.

Second, let's do more on mental health, especially for our children. When millions of young people are struggling with bullying, violence, trauma, we owe them greater access to mental health care at school.

We must finally hold social media companies accountable for the experiment they are running on our children for profit.

And it's time to pass bipartisan legislation to stop Big Tech from collecting personal data on kids and teenagers online, ban targeted advertising to children, and impose stricter limits on the personal data these companies collect on all of us.

Third, let's do more to keep our nation's one truly sacred obligation: to equip those we send into harm's way and care

for them and their families when they
come home.

Job training and job placement for
veterans and their spouses as they return
to civilian life.

Helping veterans afford their rent
because no one should be homeless in
this country, especially not those who
served it.

And we cannot go on losing 17 veterans
a day to the silent scourge of suicide.

The VA is doing everything it can,
including expanding mental health
screenings and a proven program that
recruits veterans to help other veterans

understand what they're going through and get the help they need.

And fourth, last year Jill and I re-ignited the Cancer Moonshot that President Obama asked me to lead in our Administration.

Our goal is to cut the cancer death rate by at least 50% over the next 25 years. Turn more cancers from death sentences into treatable diseases. And provide more support for patients and families.

It's personal for so many of us.

Joining us are Maurice and Kandice, an Irishman and a daughter of immigrants from Panama.

They met and fell in love in New York
City and got married in the same chapel
as Jill and I did.

Kindred spirits.

He wrote us a letter about their little
daughter Ava.

She was just a year old when she was
diagnosed with a rare kidney cancer.

26 blood transfusions. 11 rounds of
radiation. 8 rounds of chemo. 1 kidney
removed.

A 5% survival rate.

He wrote how in the darkest moments he thought, "if she goes, I can't stay."

Jill and I understand, like so many of you.

They read how Jill described our family's cancer journey and how we tried to steal moments of joy where you can.

For them, that glimmer of joy was a half-smile from their baby girl. It meant everything.

They never gave up hope.

Ava never gave up hope. She turns four next month.

They just found out that Ava beat the odds and is on her way to being cancer free, and she's watching from the White House tonight.

For the lives we can save and for the lives we have lost, let this be a truly American moment that rallies the country and the world together and proves that we can do big things.

Twenty years ago, under the leadership of President Bush and countless advocates and champions, we undertook a bipartisan effort through PEPFAR to transform the global fight against HIV/AIDS. It's been a huge success.

I believe we can do the same with cancer.

Let's end cancer as we know it and cure some cancers once and for all.

There's one reason why we're able to do all of these things: our democracy itself.

It's the most fundamental thing of all.

With democracy, everything is possible. Without it, nothing is.

For the last few years our democracy has been threatened, attacked, and put at risk.

Put to the test here, in this very room, on January 6th.

And then, just a few months ago, unhinged by the Big Lie, an assailant unleashed political violence in the home of the then-Speaker of this House of Representatives. Using the very same language that insurrectionists who stalked these halls chanted on January 6th.

Here tonight in this chamber is the man who bears the scars of that brutal attack, but is as tough and strong and as resilient as they get.

My friend, Paul Pelosi.

But such a heinous act never should have happened.

We must all speak out. There is no place for political violence in America. In America, we must protect the right to vote, not suppress that fundamental right. We honor the results of our elections, not subvert the will of the people. We must uphold the rule of the law and restore trust in our institutions of democracy.

And we must give hate and extremism in any form no safe harbor.

Democracy must not be a partisan issue. It must be an American issue.

Every generation of Americans has faced a moment where they have been called on to protect our democracy, to defend it, to stand up for it.

And this is our moment.

My fellow Americans, we meet tonight at an inflection point. One of those moments that only a few generations ever face, where the decisions we make now will decide the course of this nation and of the world for decades to come.

We are not bystanders to history. We are not powerless before the forces that confront us. It is within our power, of We the People. We are facing the test of our time and the time for choosing is at hand.

We must be the nation we have always been at our best. Optimistic. Hopeful. Forward-looking.

A nation that embraces, light over darkness, hope over fear, unity over division. Stability over chaos.

We must see each other not as enemies, but as fellow Americans. We are a good people, the only nation in the world built on an idea.

That all of us, every one of us, is created equal in the image of God. A nation that stands as a beacon to the world. A nation in a new age of possibilities.

So I have come here to fulfil my constitutional duty to report on the state of the union. And here is my report.

Because the soul of this nation is strong, because the backbone of this nation is strong, because the people of this nation are strong, the State of the Union is strong.

As I stand here tonight, I have never been more optimistic about the future of America. We just have to remember who we are.

We are the United States of America and there is nothing, nothing

beyond our capacity if we do it together.

May God bless you all. May God protect our troops.